DISCOVER THE WORLD

Empowering Children to Value Themselves, Others and the Earth

Edited by
Susan Hopkins and Jeffry Winters

Foreword by Lana Hostetler

Published in Cooperation with
Concerned Educators for a Safe Environment

New Society Publishers

Gabriola Island, BC

Philadelphia, PA

Santa Cruz, CA

Inquiries regarding requests to reprint all or part of *Discover the World: Empowering Children to Value Themselves, Others and the Earth* should be addressed to:
New Society Publishers
4527 Springfield Avenue
Philadelphia, PA 19143 USA

ISBN USA 0-86571-192-5 Paperback
ISBN USA 0-86571-191-7 Hardcover
ISBN Canada 1-55092-009-X Paperback
ISBN Canada 1-55092-008-1 Hardcover

Printed in the United States of America on partially recycled paper by Whitehall Printing Company, Wheeling, IL.

Cover design by Laurie Sandow.
Cover photo of Melina Kuchinov taken at the Friends Select School, Philadelphia, PA and published with permission.
Back cover photos: The girl, photographed by Terry Foss, was a participant in a summer youth program run by the American Friends Service Committee in Selma, AL. The boy is Carl Day Dixon, photographed by Denis Doyon.

To order directly from the publisher, add $1.75 to the price for the first copy, 50¢ for each additional. Send check or money order to:
New Society Publishers
PO Box 582
Santa Cruz, CA 95061

New Society Publishers is a project of the New Society Educational Foundation, a nonprofit, tax-exempt, public foundation. Opinions expressed in this book do not necessarily represent positions of the New Society Educational Foundation.

CONTRIBUTORS

Kathy Barnett—Teacher, Cal State Fullerton Children's Center.

Nina Bedner—Parent and Artist.

Val Buckie—Teacher and Parent.

Carol Clark—Secretary, Cal State Fullerton Children's Center.

Dave Davis, Ph.D.—Professor of Zoology and Ecology, Retired.

Connie Denholm—Teacher, CSUF Children's Center

Viki Ann Diamond—Story Teller and Folk Singer, Educational Consultant.

Susan Eaton—Educators for Social Responsibility, Orange County; Teacher, Special Education.

Abbie Enders, M.S.—Child Psychologist and Teacher of nursery school, kindergarten, first grade, and remedial reading.

Betsy Evans—Director of the Giving Tree School, Gill, MA, Teacher Trainer with High/Scope Foundation.

Betsy Gibbs—Director, Cal State Fullerton Children's Center.

Rosmarie Greiner—Founding member of CEASE, Instructor of Early Childhood Education, Workshop Leader in Peace Education.

Dorothy Hewes, Ph.D.—Professor of Early Childhood Education, San Diego State University.

Cathy Higa—Head Teacher, Cal State Fullerton Children's Center.

Lana Hostetler—Faculty member, Child Care Services, Lincoln Land Community College, Springfield, Illinois.

Susan Hopkins—Assistant Director, Cal State Fullerton Children's Center.

Tom Hunter—Freelance Songwriter, Educator, and Minstrel around issues for children, teachers, and parents.

Dolores Kirk—Peace Links, Missouri.

Susan Knox—Early Childhood Educator, President of Little Hikers, Sierra Club.

Nga Le—Teacher, Cal State Fullerton Children's Center.

Carol Loyd—Head Teacher, Cal State Fullerton Children's Center.

Janey H. Marquez—Parent, Preschool Teacher, and Teacher Trainer

Kathy Olmstead—Head Teacher, Cal State Fullerton Children's Center.

Sarah Pirtle—Author of *An Outbreak of Peace*, Parent, Musician, Teacher Trainer in conflict resolution.

Virginia Sage—Lecturer & Typist.

Viann Sanders—Teacher, Cal State Fullerton Children's Center.

Peggy Schirmer—Founder of CEASE.

Janice Sheffield—Head Teacher, Cal State Fullerton Children's Center.

Melissa Steubing—Early Childhood Educator.

Pam Steinle, Ph.D.—Parent, Lecturer in American Studies, Cal State Fullerton .

Jeffry Winters—Macintosh Enthusiast, Author, Lecturer, Consultant.

Laurie Winters—Infant Teacher, Cal State Fullerton Children's Center.

Artists—David Bedson, Sarah Clark, Blake Eddy, Sarah De Paola, Alison Rogers

DEDICATION

To all teachers and parents of young children everywhere—you play a most significant role in children's lives,

—as you model and guide peaceful problem-solving,

—as you create a climate of enthusiasm for learning about our world and its many different peoples,

—as you support each child's uniqueness.

You provide many first experiences for children, and therefore make a lasting difference in their lives.

Age 5.1
BLAKE

Table of Contents

INTRODUCTION

Not so long ago, Tom Hunter, a children's folk musician, told us of working with a group of first graders. He explained to them that he was working on a song-writing project and needed their help in telling him what children want to sing about. Together they made a long list which included such topics as dirt, shoelaces, animals, friends, popcorn, families, and a lot more. When it was time to go, he thanked them and all but one little girl left. She pulled up a chair and talked about children and music and then asked, "Can we really write songs about all these things?" Tom replied, "Sure." "It's a long list," she said. There was a long pause before she leaned closer and added, "We've got *lots* of work to do!"

What do children see and think and feel? What are the issues with which they struggle? What *do* they want to sing about? *Discover the World* contains daily activities and learning experiences designed to help children:

—develop awareness and understanding of themselves;

—develop skills in making and being friends with a wide variety of people;

—learn to communicate about their feelings, needs and problems in productive and creative ways;

—develop and deepen understanding and appreciation of themselves, others and the natural environment;

—become empowered to make the world a better place.

Fundamentally, *Discover the World* is about respect—for one's self, others, and our interconnected and fragile planet. We call this teaching of respect "peace education." In *Discover the World* we have made a special effort to integrate these concepts into concrete, hands-on activities.

Since we all learn through our entire selves, we have designed our activities to teach peace education concepts with the "whole child" in mind. Our charts of activities integrate concepts to be grasped and skills to be developed through art experience, music and movement, fine muscle and large muscle activities, and language.

The chart activities should be viewed as more than just "lesson plans." They are guides to creating an environment in which children and adults can explore, question, discover, and create. The charts have open spaces for new ideas—creativity is the basis for new solutions!

Putting together *Discover the World* has been an exciting cooperative project of people from a wide variety of experiences and life perspectives. We've come to value and respect one another as we have shared our views and confronted our differences. Our overall concern for meeting the needs of children in this complex, changing world binds us together. We hope you'll use *Discover the World* to help lead the way to creating a better world for children and for all of us.

FOREWORD

Throughout my work with young children and their families and with early childhood education professionals, one of my primary concerns has always been for the pro-social development of children. In early childhood, young children learn best with concrete hands-on activities. In their social interactions, however, we do not want them to use a literal "hands-on" approach to conflict resolution but instead encourage them to learn to express their feelings verbally and to resolve their difficulties without violence. Through concrete modeling, we teach young children to express their anger with words rather than with fists and to grow in their social competence. Through positive experiences, we strive to build in each child a strong and positive self-esteem, a trust of those around them, and the beginnings of empathy and compassion. As we assist each child in treating others fairly, as we encourage independence and decision-making by providing developmentally appropriate choices for children, and as we create a sense of community for children and their families, we are laying the foundations that will empower children to grow positively. We do this because we care about each child and we do this because we care about the society and the world. Only as our children are enabled to grow into strong, competent adults who feel a part of an integrated and peaceful world will we truly achieve the goals of enduring peace.

As a parent who marched with a toddler in the 1970 Mother's March for Peace and who then attempted to rear a peaceful man-child in an increasingly violent society, I often despaired about the proliferation of war toys and television violence while desperately seeking resources that would assist me in my child-rearing role. Similarly, as a teacher-trainer working with students preparing for careers in early childhood education, I have always sought resources that would provide concrete, developmentally appropriate activities for classroom use. Young children need our support as they grow in order to develop healthy self-esteem and a commitment to cooperation, collaboration, and the peaceful resolution of conflict.

It is especially important that we provide these experiences for today's children. While the dramatic events currently underway in Eastern Europe hopefully signal a long-term movement toward global peace, we still see an increase in violent behavior in our society. The violence in television programs continues to escalate, and new war toys, such as combat barnyard animals, continue to reach the toy market and American children. For our children to become peaceful adults, they must have experiences in their early childhood years which assist them in building the skills necessary to mature into peaceful adults. In my current travels as President of the National Association for the Education of Young Children (NAEYC), I see more and more conference attention to the issues of violence in the lives of children, to environmental awareness and safety, and to anti-bias curricular practices. Early childhood professionals recognize the vital role dealing effectively with these issues plays in the pro-social development of young children.

Discover the World: Empowering Children to Value Themselves, Others and the Earth is a valuable resource in meeting the needs of both teachers and parents for specific activities to assist them in helping children grow socially. I regret that it was not available when I was seeking resources as a parent and am delighted that it is available to both my students and to my colleagues. One of the central goals of high quality early childhood programs is to further children's growth in all domains—physical, cognitive, emotional, and social. *Discover the World* introduces children to the concepts of cooperation, collaboration, and the resolution of conflict in a peaceful manner through all four domains.

Most importantly, *Discover the World* focuses on central themes which assist young children in becoming socially competent and socially aware. By examining similarities among people, the book lays a foundation of understanding about human beings and their commonalities and a foundation of understanding about our human responsibilities for one another and for the resources of our small planet. At the same time, *Discover the World* stresses both the importance of multi-cultural experiences infused throughout the curriculum and the need to provide experiences which enable each child to understand his or her uniqueness and to build self-esteem.

My son, who once rode in a stroller in peace marches, now marches as an adult arm-in-arm with others committed to preserving our environment and global resources. One of my former students working with children makes a "friendship" bread and provides materials for friendship art whenever she sees tension and conflict building in the classroom. For both of them, it was necessary for me to develop my own resources to further their growth. For my students today, however, *Discover the World* is an excellent resource to help all of us meet our mutual goals of furthering the growth of children and the society toward a peaceful and healthy world for all humankind.

Lana L. Hostetler
Lincoln Land Community College
Springfield, Illinois

SELF–AWARENESS

by Janice Sheffield

Self–Esteem

Children need to become aware of how special they are in order to develop high self-esteem. When children have high self–esteem, they are better able to express their feelings and thoughts. When children and adults learn to use their words to express how they are feeling, there will be fewer pent-up hostilities. Perhaps we would have a better understanding of others and of peace if all of us learned to problem-solve in ways that lead us to higher self–esteem.

Sarah DePaola
Age 4.4

Self Esteem Chart

Self-Esteem

by Janice Sheffield

Concept	I'm me, I'm special. There is no one else just like me.	Each of us is special.	I can use my words to express my feelings and thoughts.	I am capable. I can do lots of things.	We are all special so let's celebrate together.
Art Experience	Fingerpaint—at the end make a print of child's hands.	Paint a mural—hang on wall when dry.		Stringing: use cheerios, paper shapes, pieces of straw.	
Science Experience	Weigh and measure children. Have a string the same height as the child so he/she can measure other things.		Make tin can telephone and use it.	Magnet play—try to get paper clips out of water without touching the water.	Cook a snack together and then eat.
Music and Movement	"Magic Penny" "I Have Feelings"	"Magic Penny" (hugs, kisses)	Simon Says: do body parts—touch elbow, touch toes, touch nose.	"I Have Feelings"	"Magic Penny" "I Have Feelings"
Fine Muscle	Beauty shop—make up, rollers, etc. Use cold cream to remove after play.	Cut out basic person shape to decorate.		Magnet play.	
Large Muscle		Blocks/large trucks.	Playdough.		Dancing with scarves to music.
Language	Tape record children telling what they like to do.	Describe someone by how they look—guess who.	I am happy when ____. I feel sad when ____.	Share a special trick or stunt.	
Special Activities	Children's photographs are on the wall for them to see all week.		Teachers role play settling a dispute over a toy (or anything) by verbalizing feelings and negotiating.		Have a picnic lunch outside together.

I HAVE FEELINGS (song)

Chorus:
I feel just right in the skin I wear,
There's no one like me anywhere.
I feel just right in the skin I wear,
There's no one like me anywhere.

1. I have feelings and you do too.
I'd like to share a few with you.
Sometimes I'm happy and sometimes I'm sad,
Sometimes I'm scared, and sometimes mad,
The most important feeling you see,
Is that I'm proud of being me.   Chorus

2. No one sees the things I see, behind my eyes is only me.
And no one knows where my feelings begin
There's only me inside my skin.
No one does what I can do,
I'll be me, and you be you.   Chorus

Source Unknown

MAGIC PENNY

Love is something if you (give it away) repeat twice
Love is something if you give it away
You'll end up having more.
It's just like a magic penny
Hold on tight and you won't have any
Lend it, spend it and you'll have so many
They'll roll all over the floor.

—Repeat first three lines

A hug is something . . .
A smile is something . . .

Words and Music by Malvina Reynolds
©Copyright 1955, 1959 by Northern Music Corporation, New York, NY 10019.
Rights administered by MCA Music Publishing, A Division of MCA, Inc.
Used by permission

Girls and Boys—What Am I? Chart

Girls and Boys—What Am I?

by Janey Marquez and Susan Hopkins

	Boys and girls share many abilities.	Girls and boys both contribute to our world. (Women)	(Men)	Boys and girls share the same feelings and emotions.	Girls and boys have some physical differences.	Boys and girls work together to make our world a better place.
Art Experience	Clay available for all children.	Mary Cassatt—painter	Charles Schultz—cartoonist	Paint with various colors and discuss the feelings the colors make you feel.	Collage of pictures of boys and pictures of girls.	Friendship painting—a group art project.
Science Experience	Science experiments available for all children.	Sally Ride—astronaut	Andy Lipkis—Tree People		Use of adult terminology for penis and vagina.	
Music and Movement	Dancing and singing for all children.	Tracy Chapman—singer	Mikhail Baryshnikov—ballet dancer	"If You're Happy and You Know It"		Use of partners in movement such as "Row, Row, Row Your Boat."
Fine Muscle	Sewing and weaving for all children.	Susie Yazzie—Navaho weaver	Paul Saufkie—Hopi weaver	Make masks of various feelings.		Cooperative collage.
Large Muscle	All children practice running, jumping, hopping, tumbling, playing ball, etc.	Mary Lou Retton—gymnast	Kareem Abdul-Jabbar—basketball	Pantomime how you move your body when you feel happy, sad, mad, etc.		Community block building.
Language	Discuss concept that all people are capable.	Charlotte Zolotow—children's book author	Don Freeman—children's book author	Read and discuss *William's Doll* by Charlotte Zolotow.	Read and discuss *What is a Boy? What is a Girl?* by Waxman.	Discuss specific situations where boys and girls have worked together.
Special Activities	Discuss how the people in your family help do all the work.			Have dolls available to care for and use in dramatic play.	Video: *Free to Be You and Me* by Marlo Thomas (hospital dialogue).	Cooking—everyone contribute to the outcome.

<u>Feelings</u>

by Susan Hopkins

One of the most wonderful and special things about young children is their ability to be real, to be genuine—to show how they are feeling about the events and people in their lives. Their openness is one of their most charming characteristics. Generally, most young children will let us know clearly when they are happy, sad, angry, or otherwise. Sometimes their expression of feelings may be inappropriate—after all, they are very young. This becomes an opportunity for us to support the feelings expressed, model productive ways to cope with the feelings, and then help children learn to express their feelings in ways which will help them grow in self–esteem.

When working with young children, certain communication techniques are very helpful in supporting them. One can use the following techniques to help children verbalize feelings:

—listening quietly
—simple acknowledgment "uh-huh", "really"
—door openers—"I'd like to hear about it."
—active listening.

We will find children, and all people, much more willing to share their feelings when we support them with quality listening. Avoidance of techniques such as shaming, moralizing, preaching, ordering, blaming, judging, name-calling, admonishing, and advising are also critically important.

Secondly, the use of "I Messages" in contrast to "You Messages" will support the development of high self–esteem through modeling appropriate expression of feelings. For example, "I'm feeling tired and rushed. I need your help" in contrast to, "You are lazy." We create positive interactions with young children when we model appropriate techniques for expressing our feelings. These interactions will be one of the most important gifts we can share with children. They will learn to express their feelings in productive, positive ways if we will listen, support, and share words and techniques with them that express feelings appropriately.

Feelings Chart

Feelings
by Susan Hopkins

Concept	I have lots of different feelings: happy, sad, angry, etc.	Sometimes I feel angry.	There are lots of ways I can show and tell how I feel.	When my friend is feeling sad, I can try to help.	If I try very hard, I can do lots of things.
Art Experience		Mad Paintings	Make feelings masks	Make a picture or gift for a friend.	Make scenery for the play.
Science Experience					
Music and Movement	Hap Palmer: "Everybody Has Feelings"	Run in an angry way; in a gentle way.	Song: "If You're Happy and You Know It."	Musical Hugs: Play music—stop music & hug the nearest person.	
Fine Muscle	Draw pictures of sad things, happy things, etc. and make a book.				Make costumes for the play.
Large Muscle	Adults pantomime feelings, then children take turns.	Hammer; punch playdough.	Children pantomime various feelings.		Practice working together to be like trains.
Language	Feelings words: sad, happy, angry, mad, frustrated, loving, peaceful, etc.	David Was Mad by Bill Martin.	Talking Without Words by Marie Hall Ets.	Practice listening when someone is talking.	Read: The Little Engine That Could by Watty Piper.
Special Activities	Feelings Various stories by Charlotte Zolotow.	Role play ways to vent anger productively.	Role play telling people how you feel.		Act out The Little Engine that Could with no audience.

Activities for Infants and Toddlers

Activities to Help Infants and Toddlers
Value Peace, Empathy, and Cooperation

by Kathy Olmstead

Peaceful, able, supportive people are not just born that way. Each experience an infant has impacts that child's impression of what the world should be like. If the people babies value most are cool, brisk, and uninvolved, a child is inclined to model that behavior. Treating children with warmth, attention, and concern offers them more opportunities to develop as caring, nurturing human beings.

Our day-to-day interactions with babies and toddlers should reinforce the things we think are important for them to learn. We can also spend time doing special things with them, focused towards development of those ideas.

The following concepts are important:

1. Peaceful is a good feeling;

2. People should often be joyful;

3. There are all kinds of people in the world;

4. People have all kinds of feelings;

5. People can learn to be peaceful and gentle with each other;

6. People can help each other;

7. Helping each other can make an experience easier and more rewarding.

These concepts can be fostered, using a variety of activity areas such as:

A. Social-Emotional

B. Sensory-Science

C. Fine Muscle

D. Gross Muscle

E. Music-Movement

F. Language

At the end of each of the following activities is a set of numbers and letters that refer back to the concepts supported (i.e., 1. Peaceful is a good feeling) and the activity area utilized (i.e., C. Fine Muscle).

Activities

Touch babies with pieces of soft material (e.g., scraps of fur, flannel, etc.) while talking softly and lovingly.   [1;A,B,F]

Put one or two babies underneath and near the middle of a parachute or king-size sheet and lift and lower the material softly, making it billow softly around the children.   [1;A,B]

Take a child in your arms. Put on soft music and dance gently.   [1,5;A,E]

Take a child in your arms. Put on a bouncy, happy rhythm, and dance joyfully.   [2;A,E]

Play "Mousie." Lay a baby down on her back and "creep" your fingers (like a mouse creeping) on the baby's body, identifying the body part as you go. For instance, "Now mousie is creeping on your shoulder." [5;A,B,F]

Lie a baby down in the middle of a strong, rectangular piece of cloth or blanket. Have two kneeling adults pick up two ends and begin to lift the child up about a foot off the ground, swinging the cloth gently, talking softly to the baby. [5;A,D,F]

Inflate an inner tube. Sit the child on it facing towards you. Hold the child gently but firmly and bounce her up and down, smiling and laughing together. [2;A,D]

Build a "mountain" of big and little pillows and encourage a child to crawl up and around and over it. Help the child lay down on the top and roll gently down the sides. [5;D]

Sit with a child in your lap and look together into a mirror. Make faces—happy, sad, surprised, angry—identifying feelings to the baby (e.g., "Look at my happy face. I feel happy.") [4;A,B,F]

Cut large, simple pictures out of magazines of people of many races and cultures. Make a picture file, one picture on each page. Mix in many different expressions. Sit with a baby in your lap and talk about each picture. [3,4;A,F]

Gather a number of soft toys and have the toddler help you put them into a box. Talk with her about gentle touching and helping each other. When the toys are all in the box, dump the box over together, letting the toys spill out, saying "Ta Da!" Repeat. [6,7;C,F]

Wrap a number of soft things in tissue paper (toys, stuffed animals, etc.) and ask a child to help you do some "work" unwrapping these things. Identify each item as it is unwrapped. [6,7;A,C,F]

Drop a number of things (cards, pegs, etc.) onto the ground. Ask "Who can help me pick these up?" Reward the child verbally for helping. [6,7;A,C]

Play a game with a child who is very active. When you are done, sit down together and hug each other and talk about how good it feels to be peaceful together. [1;A,C,F]

Set a doll or large stuffed toy in a small chair with another child-size chair facing it. Offer a child a bib, a spoon, and a bowl, and encourage him to feed his "baby." Talk about people taking care of each other. [6;A,C,F]

Provide a child with a deep tub, filled part way with soapy water. Add plastic baby dolls and sponges. Talk with the child about washing the "babies" gently and helping make them clean and comfortable. Provide towels, and help the child dry the dolls gently. [6,7;A,B,C]

Books to Enjoy with Infants and Toddlers

Appropriate for Both Infants and Toddlers = B, Appropriate for Toddlers = T

Author	Level	Book Title
Bang, Molly	B	*Ten Nine Eight*
Battaglia, Aurelius	B	*Animal Sounds*
Brown, Margaret Wise	T	*Good Night Moon* *Home for a Bunny* *Runaway Bunny*
Calmenson, Stephanie	B	*Babies*
Crews, Donald	T	*Freight Train*
Degen, Bruce	T	*Jamberry*
Ets, Marie Hall	T	*Play With Me*
Field , Eugene	T	*Wynken, Blynken and Nod*
Greely, Vallerie	T	*Pets*
Gretz, Susanna	T	*I'm Not Sleepy* *Ready for Bed*
Hayes, Sarah	T	*Eat Up Gemma*
Hoban, Tana	T	*Of Colors and Things* *Shapes and Things*
Jonas, Ann	T	*Where Can It Be?*
Krauss, Ruth	T	*The Carrot Seed* *The Happy Egg*
Lynn, Sara	B	*Big Animals* *Clothes* *Farm Animals* *Food* *Garden Animals* *Toys*
McMillian, Bruce	T	*Growing Colors*
Merriam, Eve	T	*Mommies at Work*
Miller, Margaret	B	*At My House* *In My Room* *Me and My Clothes* *My First Words* *Time to Eat*
O'Brian, Anne Sibley	T	*Come Play with Us*
Oxenbury, Helen	B	*All Fall Down* *Clap Hands* *Say Good Night* *Tickle, Tickle*
Pellegrino, Virginia	B	*Listen to the City* *Listen to the Country*

Social Responsibility Chart

Social Responsibility by Kathy Barnett

Concept	Children everywhere like to take care of themselves.	Animals need our help in taking care of them.	As a member of a family I share in the chores at home.	I am important at school. I can help.	Children are able to take care of their surroundings. "I am a part of the whole world."
Art Experience		Create a picture of home pet or design a pet you would like to have.	Decorate aprons to use at home or school.		Make posters to encourage recycling.
Science Experience	Accept responsibility for school pets for one week.		Make celery & peanut butter for snack so children can make it at home for family.		Recycling.
Music and Movement	Sing "This is the Way We Brush Our Teeth" song. Tune: "Here We Go Round the Mulberry Bush."			In small groups, help with feeding babies in school infant program.	"This Land is Your Land" by Woody Guthrie.
Fine Muscle		Children glue pictures of pets from home or made at school onto a background & post in classroom.	Painting on aprons.	Clean classroom toys. Pair up and wash each others hands.	Glue pictures & trash to recycling poster to hang up at school.
Large Muscle			Use aprons for dramatic play in housekeeping area.	Dispose of school trash.	Pick up trash in environment surrounding your center.
Language	Read stories about what we do to help ourselves (brush teeth, dress, etc.).	Bring pictures of pets from home.	Make a class list of jobs children do at home.		Talk about recycling & put children's thoughts about it on poster.
Special Activities		Read *Thy Friend, Obadiah* by Brinton Turkle.	Read *She Come Bringing Me That Little Baby Girl* by Eloise Greenfield.		

Awareness of Space Chart

Awareness of Space by Dave Davis

Concept	Our bodies take up space.	Other people need space too.	Too many people in too small a place causes problems: not enough food, fighting for things.	We need space to feel comfortable.
Art Experience	Paint on large paper and on small paper.	Paint on paper from which center has been removed.	Collage using large items on small paper and then using small items on large paper.	Collage using large paper with lots of choices.
Science Experience			Provide a very small amount of food for many children to eat. Gradually increase the number of goldfish in a bowl—see how they can barely swim.	Provide enough snack for everyone.
Music and Movement	Position body in different ways to take up a little and lots of space.	Move around room without touching other people.	Move about room with a couple of children without touching—add children until it is crowded. Crowd many children into a small place to see how it feels.	
Fine Muscle	Do body tracings. Color in body tracings.		Color providing limited number of crayons. Problem-solve not enough to go around.	Provide at least one crayon for each child.
Large Muscle	Jumping, hopping, etc., within a given space, large & small.	Move in one space—move all around.	See Ann & Paul Barlin, *Learning Through Movement*, for spacial awareness ideas.	Create obstacle courses with the children.
Language			Discussion: How does it feel to be crowded? What happens when people are too crowded? Discussion: What can we do when the "block corner" becomes too crowded?	Discuss the feelings of being too crowded versus having enough space.
Special Activities	*The Garden of One* by Sharon Rice			

Friends

    Through friends we learn that people are more alike than different. When people can see how much others are like them, they begin to care, to understand, to love.

Age 3.8
Alison Rogers

Friends Chart 1

Friends #1   by Janice Sheffield

Concept	It is fun to make new friends.	Friends like to be called by their names.	Friends are people we especially like to be with.	I can have many friends.	I can have friends at home and at school.
Art Experience	Large collage for everyone to work on all week long.	Add something new to collage.		Use leaves, twigs, etc. that were found on field trip to add to the collage.	Add something new for collage. Paint collage.
Science Experience	Have the children help clean the animal cage.		Field trip to gather leaves, twigs, to add to collage.	Water play.	
Music and Movement	"The More we get Together"	"It's a Small World"		"Mousercise"	
Fine Muscle		Children fish for fish-shaped name tags then find the owner (teacher read name).			Paint.
Large Muscle			Go for a walk with friends.	Everyone take off one shoe, put in pile. Get one shoe and find the owner.	Parachute play.
Language	Chant: I'm your neighbor, how do you do? I am _____, who are you?	Puppets—one puppet can't remember names. Children help when the puppet asks.	Share one favorite find from field trip.	Who is it? Have child describe someone and have children guess who it is.	Read a book together.
Special Activities	Go outside in pairs—holding hands with a buddy. Use all senses pointing out things of interest.			Have a friendship tree— a tree with children's pictures on it.	

Friends Chart 2

Friends Chart #2   by Cathy Higa

	Friends work together through sharing and contributing. "Friendship Fruit Salad"	Friends work together and enjoy each other.	Friends call each other by their names.	Friends help to keep their classroom/school safe. Children take a "clean up walk" around school.	Friends do special things for each other.
Concept					
Art Experience	Print with fruits and paint. Children can associate who brought which fruit.		Texture Names: sprinkle sand, rice, etc. over glue traced names. Name Hats: children decorate.	Odds-n-ends collage—children use "found junk" to create. Ex. plastic wrap, feathers, paper, etc.	Children draw pictures for a sick friend. Children draw on a birthday child's crown.
Science Experience	Examine seeds, compare/contrast skin, smell, taste, etc. Preparation of Fruit Salad.	Play "Mirrors" game. Children face each other and try to copy movements through leader/follower.		Safety Hunt—Children look for unsafe toys/conditions. Ex. Broken plastic cup.	
Music and Movement	Children can pretend to be a seed and grow into fruit tree. Observe the orchard of "Fruit Friends."	"Row, Row, Row Your Boat" Children sit facing partner; match hands & feet— push & pull with the song.	Sing name songs—ex. "Where's Joel?" "Whenever Mike Has His Green Shirt On" Clap rhythm of child's name: i.e. Ni-cole Al-cain		Children teach their friends a new song. The teacher can dictate the words.
Fine Muscle	Cut, peel, stir the fruit salad.	String beads together. One child holds string and the other puts beads/cereal onto it.			Helping Hands: A child takes a project home to fix with family, then brings back to school. Examples: books, toy, etc.
Large Muscle		Square Dancing to "Old Brass Wagon.." Children link arms, twirl each other, and bow.	Play a "Who's Missing" game for attendance. Play a name-riddle game: "This friend is wearing jeans and has a red car. Who is it?"	Clean up walk around school or classroom.	
Language	Provide a sign-up chart. Children choose what they want to contribute and see child-fruit association.	Create a "My Friends Book" Children draw self portraits and dictate special stories of self. Create a "How I Can Be A Friend" book. Children draw and dictate story.		Create a classroom book: "Friends Take Care of Their Classroom." Children draw and dictate.	
Special Activities	Chart: Apples = John, Bananas = Lisa, Grapes = Michelle, Pineapple = Ryan		Post a class picture at children's eye level. "Can You Name Your Friends?" Name all the children.	Play problem-solving games. "What would you do if you saw a puzzle outside?"	Children assist an injured friend. Example: Wipe friend's bumped elbow. Help to rinse paint out of a friend's shirt.

Friends with Physical or Mental Limitations

by Kathy Barnett

In the community there is a variety of interesting people; people who deliver mail, collect garbage, care for babies, work in offices. Just as these people perform their jobs differently, people's bodies work in different ways. Children can be frightened by these differences, or they can view them with understanding, depending upon how adult role models approach the subject.

When talking about people who have physical or mental limitations, the emphasis should be upon what each person can do; how they are valuable and contributing members of the community.

Too easily the value of a person gets lost in a "label." When referring to people who are different in any way, a rule to remember is "People First." For example, "My friend with glasses or a student in a wheelchair." At our school, Sylvia, a young woman who is developmentally delayed, works in the kitchen. Although the children can recognize that Sylvia is different, more importantly, she is known as the person who washes the dishes.

Our children receive a valuable lesson on the importance of each person as they become aware of different people working and playing together at school and home. Integration of people who are disabled as well as able is the best way for all to become familiar with each other.

Exploring all aspects of the larger world is always interesting to young children. Facilitating the introduction between groups who may not already know each other is an important opportunity afforded each caregiver.

Adaptive equipment you can use in your classroom includes, but is not limited to:

wheelchairs
canes
braille writers
hearing aids
braces
communication boards or wallets (boards/wallets with pictures of things or activities a person who communicates without verbal language might need or want, e.g., bike, toilet, food, toy, etc.).

Awareness of Others Chart

Awareness of Others   by Kathy Barnett

Concept	People who can't see can do many, many things.	People who can't hear communicate in other ways.	People who can't walk get around in other ways.	People who can't talk communicate in different ways.	All people can learn to do important things.
Art Experience	Pudding paint while blindfolded.		Have a variety of art activities. Point out that you can do this activity no matter how you get around.	Each child construct (cut, glue) a "communication wallet" to show pictures of needed items.	
Science Experience	Taste, smell, feel pudding.	Plug ears & guess what others are saying.	Explore wheelchairs, canes, crutches.		
Music and Movement	Close your eyes & dance.	Sing a song while signing it.	Do a wheelchair dance!	Communicate with music across room using instruments instead of voices.	
Fine Muscle	Feely box	Sign language		Cut out pictures for "communication wallets"; glue in books.	Put one hand behind back and try to do tasks. Wear a patch over one eye.
Large Muscle	One at a time with teacher's help, walk, blindfolded, from group time to activity table.	Play "Simon Says" without making any sounds.	Alternative ways to get around: experiment with crab walk, rolling, scooting, crawling.		
Language	Experience a book written in braille.	Sign language—songs, stories, everyday activities.	Note & discuss slight handicaps that our friends have—glasses, braces, hearing aids, etc.	Work with "communication boards" to show pictures to express needs.	Talk about different jobs that need to be done each day. How can everyone help out?
Special Activities	Visit handicapped community center to explore, experience adaptive equipment.	Story: *Lisa and Her Soundless World* by Edna S. Levine.	Each child take a turn spending about 10 min. experiencing everyday activities from wheelchair.		Visit handicapped community center to return equipment.

Friends of All Ages

by Val Buckie

Teaching children about people of different age groups is an important part of becoming aware of others. A life cycle lesson can help children be comfortable with people who are different ages than themselves.

Teaching children about the following concepts may help to engage children in thinking about age:

1. Babies —why babies cry; how they experience the world; how much preschoolers have learned since they were babies; how to care for babies.

2. Children—the rights and responsibilities children have for themselves and their surroundings.

3. Teenagers—half–way to adulthood.

4. Adults—act out what children think adults do, such as careers, homemaking, shopping, and parenting.

5. Senior Citizens—talk about wisdom, life experience in the old days before T.V. etc.. Discuss some of the processes of aging such as wrinkles, brittle bones, loneliness, illness, and death if appropriate. Retirement can be emphasized as a positive life experience which includes time for hobbies, enjoying families, etc..

It is important to invite visitors into the classroom to participate in or demonstrate activities. Remember to make lasting friendships with these people by taking their pictures and putting them up in the classroom. It's wonderful to continue to correspond with them.

Helping Hands

by Carol Loyd

Young children learn that their hands can help in many ways. They begin by helping themselves, around their home environments, with adults, and in the community. Children begin to identify with others in a positive way when they are working together toward a common goal. An example would be a newspaper drive from which they are able to keep the money and decide together how it should be spent. It is important that we support children in such endeavors so they can begin to realize the value of each individual's contribution to society in making our world a more efficiently functioning and happier place to live.

<u>Helping Hands Chart</u>

Helping Hands by Carol Loyd

Concept	Children learn different ways to help around their environment.	Children discover ways of helping in the adult world.	Children learn to work together to achieve a common goal.	Children learn to help out in the community.	Children learn that they can be rewarded by cleaning up the environment. (newspaper drive)
Art Experience	All work together to build a play store.	Handprint painting.	Make soap bubble prints.	Make newspaper drive signs (print, color).	Continue newspaper drive. Make a newspaper collage.
Science Experience	Bake "Hand" cookies for "sale" in play store.	Children learn how to feel for pulse rate—resting & active.	Soap and milk experiment. Add food-colored soap to cold milk. Watch design.	Try "bleaching" newspaper with lemon juice or vinegar & sunshine.	Fingerpaint on children's "bleached" newspaper.
Music and Movement	"Clap, Clap, Clap Your Hands"	Sesame Street exercise tape.	"We Are the World"	"The People on the Bus"	"We've Got the Whole World in Our Hands"
Fine Muscle	Paint, cut, glue pieces/items for store.	Wind bandages, administering "shots," listening to heartbeats.	Help wash smaller toys and separate into groups.	Paint newspaper drive signs.	Use hands to help.
Large Muscle	Obstacle course—holding hands!	Dress up—act out "rescues" 911 emergency #	Wash chairs, table, toys.	Collect newspapers (carrying, lifting, moving).	Pick up trash around school.
Language	Identify objects for sale in play store.	Discuss good health ideas.	Discuss how working together can be fun!	Take a guided tour through a recycling center.	Show and discuss different items which are made from recycled newspapers (phone books, etc.).
Special Activities	Dramatic play "store."	Dramatic play "doctor, nurse, hospital."	Make a "get well" book for a sick friend.	Help bring newspapers to recycling center.	Children get to help pick out new items for center or home purchased with money earned through recycling.

Hunger

by Kathy Barnett

In addressing the challenge of hunger with young children, a few issues need to be considered:

1. This is not a time to do art projects with food (macaroni, beans, etc.).

2. Care should be taken not to frighten the children about "starving children."

3. Beware of falling into a superior attitude. "Those poor, starving children" can elicit pity instead of understanding.

4. For young children, the concept of sharing food seems most appropriate when the child has enough to eat. A hungry child cannot be expected to share, but when it comes to "seconds" a child could be asked to consider the needs of others who also may want more.

5. Sharing is a most difficult concept for young children. We can work with it in terms of helping others (i.e., making something for a friend who is sick), but not when it comes to sharing toys. In respect to toys, the concept of "taking turns" is far more appropriate: "After John's turn on the bike is finished, you may have a turn."

This study of hunger may take longer, or could be spread out over several months, because of the food drive and gardening ideas.

Hunger Chart

Hunger by Kathy Barnett

Concept	Good nutrition involves eating a balanced diet of various foods.	We can grow food.	Not everyone has as much food as they would like.	Sharing means giving of ourselves to help others (see notes).	We can share food with our neighbors.
Art Experience		Paint pictures of garden.			
Science Experience	Make a food group mural. Hang in eating area.	Have a drought in one part of the garden. What happens?	Discuss with the group that sometimes people don't have enough food. Then have a snack with only one serving per child. Afterwards discuss: Did you want more? How did it feel not to be able to have more?	Share garden work.	Make bread together. See "Breads Around the World." Send recipe home.
Music and Movement		"Inch by inch, row by row - gotta make this garden grow ..." (Viki Diamond Tape)			
Fine Muscle	Cut out pictures of foods for mural, pasting.	Plant seeds.		Make a salad from garden produce to share with others.	Each child kneads a small amount of bread dough and adds it to class loaf.
Large Muscle		Cultivate the soil.			
Language	Discuss food groups and "balanced diet."	Discuss seeds to be sown. Contrast mature fruits and vegetables.		Discuss taking your portion of food and leaving enough for others (see notes).	Vocabulary - label food and put cans in categories. Make a grocery store in classroom.
Special Activities	Conduct a food drive this week. Ask families to bring in dried and canned foods to donate to a local food bank.	Start a garden.	Problem-solve: We have one piece of watermelon and 4 children want it. What shall we do?		Pack up food with children to send to the food bank.

CONFLICT MANAGEMENT

Conflict Management as a Part of the Peace Curriculum

by Susan Hopkins

Conflict is a reality in everyone's life. While many people may wish to avoid it as something unpleasant, which it can be if handled inappropriately, it is important to help people face conflict and learn how to deal with it in productive, nonviolent ways. This is not to say that one should go about encouraging conflict, but when it occurs naturally, attempt to work with it to build practice in problem–solving.

It is important to help young children learn the processes of problem–solving which include verbalizing feelings, communicating what the problem is, creating several solutions, discussing solutions, making a choice, trying out possible solutions, and evaluating the results. Children as well as adults need much practice in skills such as verbalizing, listening, remembering, making choices, and following through. These are critical life skills and it is our responsibility to encourage and support the children and adults in our environments in using them.

The following guide may be useful in supporting people in conflict management. The steps are listed in sequence and if one will practice using them regularly with children they should become routine in the course of managing conflicts. As with many learning experiences, it will not be easy at first, but is so important that the effort is certainly worthwhile. When, at some point, a child comes up to you and says, "We've got a problem, and this is what it is . . . ," you'll know you're making real progress in the area of peaceful conflict management.

Steps to Managing Conflict

I. Defuse Anger

Anger is such an intense feeling that it must be defused before any negotiation can happen. Supportive, active listening may help, pounding the playdough may help, hugs may help. (Using everyday songs in new, simple ways can also help: "Gee I'm mad, skip to my Loo . . .") There are many productive ways to defuse anger.

II. Listen to People's Feelings

Help children become aware of their own feelings, as well as those of others, by listening to and reflecting the feelings expressed. Acknowledge and support the feelings; after all, the feelings are real and it is critical that we pay close attention to what the children express to us. Their feelings must be validated.

III. Problem solve

Once anger is defused and feelings are respected, then one can settle into problem-solving. Help the children:

> A. Collect information: "What happened?"
> B. State the problem clearly, including everyone's needs.
> C. Think of solutions.
> D. Look at possible consequences of the solutions.
> E. Plan the solution and help implement as needed.

Supporting children's growth using this guide will help them become negotiators in conflict management and will encourage their independence. As they learn to problem-solve they will need less adult intervention and they will grow in confidence.

<u>Conflict Resolution Ideas for Ages 3-5</u>

by Betsy Evans and Sarah Pirtle

As we think about children between the ages of three and five, we can identify these developmental issues:

• Their learning occurs in small bits.

• They are working on realizing their separation from their parents.

• The children are physically expressive, and they learn in active ways.

• Their difficulties result from trying to understand the world from physical cues only.

• They are still intensely egocentric.

• They have a limited understanding of how they affect the world and other people.

• Consequently, they need to constantly experiment with control over their world.

• Their fears result from immature understanding of the world and their own impact on people and events.

We find this a helpful backdrop as we look at children's efforts to resolve conflict and as we identify the types of assistance we can give them.

<u>Planning for Children's Needs: Conflict Prevention</u>

Here are three ways teachers and parents can prevent conflicts.

1) **Establishing a consistent routine and communicating it clearly.**
   Children need concrete ways to look at a routine. Families and schools can find ways to do this which are other than verbal, such as using pictorial symbols on calendars or charts. For example, at the Giving Tree School we have taken photographs of children at different times of the day and have mounted them on poster board. Now, when a child asks, "Is it time for my Mommy to come yet?" we can look at the chart together and talk about what part of the day we are in and what will happen next. The stages of our school day include:
   Greeting,
   Planning,
   Choices,
   Recall and small group,
   Circle, and
   Outside.

Children know what each part of the routine means, have the names of these stages in their vocabulary, and count upon this sequence as a consistent structure of time.

2) **Plan together for changes.**

When a teacher had to be away from school for five days, she asked the children, "How can I show you how long I'll be away?" They decided balloons would be the symbol. Five balloons were blown up and one was popped as each day until she returned.

When a parent has to be gone from the home, a calendar to mark the days helps make the passage of time concrete. Another method is to make letter cards, one for each day absent that spell a message when you turn them over. The secret word, decoded day be day, might be "popcorn" with a popcorn treat on the day the missed parent or teacher comes back.

If parents are divorced and children spend time in two households with different schedules, charts can help create the pictures to help orient to the differences. A child who likes to draw can help create the pictures to represent the various activities.

Using sequence charts or lists, children are able to predict what is coming next and plan and prepare for it. If changes are physically shown, they can feel more certain they will happen.

3)   **Establish realistic rules and give reasons for them.**

Children are ready to follow rules when they are clear and simple, when they are easy to remember and understand. They also appreciate boundaries for their behavior. An authoritarian relationship is removed once children understand the reasons.

At school we never use the word, "rule," per se, but focus on routines, expectations, and responsibilities. One child said to his mother, "We don't have rules at school. When they say 'no' to us, they just tell us the reasons."

Reasons are a crucial part of the communication. These can be phrased, in fact, in terms of options: rather than saying to a child, "Don't run into that puddle!" a more useful communication would be, "If you run into that puddle, your shoes are going to feel very wet, and you might feel uncomfortable later," because the reasons are both evident and personalized.

If children have difficulty following a rule, ask them if there is something about it they don't understand.

A visual reminder helps children to respect physical boundaries. If children can ride a bike only a certain distance, a painted line is a more effective way for them to understand the rule than the words, "Don't go too far."

At school there is a rope between two trees in the playground to indicate how far they can walk in that corner of the yard. Unlike a fence, it is a boundary they could actually step over, but they keep the agreement and use it as a reminder. During the winter, when a trapeze hangs inside, a piece of tape on the rug shows where children need to stand so that they won't be hit by it while another person is swinging. In these ways rules are concretely elucidated,

These three recommendations speak to children's needs for concrete representation, and clear simple communication.

Intervention: Assisting Children in Problem Solving

Here are three more ideas on how to foster the kinds of communication which are building blocks for conflict resolution.

1)   **Give support. Offer encouragement instead of praise.**

Consider two different ways to respond when a child shares a new painting. One approach might be to say, "That's really beautiful." Another is to use observations, like "I see lots of red," and open-ended questions such as, "Can you tell me about that big circle on the top?" This is the difference between praise and encouragement. Praise stops the conversation, reinforces products, and attaches children to adult judgements. Encouragement opens up a dialogue, reinforces process, and builds self esteem.

Switching to this mode of communication may be an unlearning process for those of us who grew up hearing adults respond with praise. It takes work and may feel unfamiliar at first, but asking questions like "How did you make that?" or "What are those long lines reaching toward that box?" fosters a rich, satisfying dialog with children.

Open-ended questions also provide a foundation for problem-solving. As we try to solve conflicts there is not one right answer. There is not one phrase which needs to be learned and repeated. Rather, we approach conflicts as an *inventive process* because they require that we explore together, through negotiation, our unique solution or common agreement.

As adults going into conflict resolution, it is important that we don't decide ahead of time how the result "should" go. When we talk with children about their problem solving efforts we use open-ended questions for encouragement. For example, we can ask a child who is working on a conflict with another, "What have you tried so far?" or "Can you think of another way to do this?" Open-ended questions support active learning.

2)   Acknowledge feelings.

Children do things for a reason. As adults we can stop and think why children are doing what they are doing. People want most of all for others to know what they are feeling.

We try not to state the feeling too soon or label the reason for the emotion. For example, if a child walks into lunch at the end of the line with a sad expression, a teacher might guess he or she is feeling upset because of being last, but a response of "It looks to me like you're sad" can be enough for the child to know that their feelings are understood and respected.

When we ask ourselves—what is this child telling me?—and reflect back to them what we observe, we communicate that their feelings are the healthy part of them that experiences the world. We let them know that we have joined them where they are.

3)   Offer alternatives, give openings, avoid power struggles.

At those moments when we expect that children may have difficulty, we can express our expectations in a form that gives options. For example, rather than telling a child, "Go clean up now!," the statement, "Before you have dinner you need to pick up your Legos and put them in the red basket," presents dinner as an option and gives specific information on what needs to be cleaned up and where it needs to go.

We can be direct in our statements and at the same time give choices and reasons. For example, "You are using such a loud voice that I can't hear. Either use a soft voice or choose a different place to play." Or, "Cutting the pages of the book is not a choice because we could not read it after it has been cut. You *can* cut this paper over here."

This method of giving choices helps to make a situation concrete. For example, we can respond to a child who is feeling upset by asking, "What would you like to have happen right now?" Then she or he can choose whether holding the teacher's hand, or sitting quietly reading a book, or having support in joining the circle of children will be personally helpful.

These communication guidelines help us engage with children and help them learn how to engage with their peers. Engagement is a key concept in working with conflicts.

Conflict Resolution Techniques

Here is the sequence we find handy to keep in mind when we as adults assist children in handling conflicts.

1)   **Listen and observe** the problem so that you can assess what it is and whether you should intervene. Consider all the various stresses a child may be feeling: changes in family routine, illness, different levels of competence between siblings or friends. Observe what is happening before you step in. If behavior that is unsafe or destructive is going on, intervene immediately.

2) Help children **stop and think**.
   Sometimes holding the hands of the children involved can give reassurance. Or just a thoughtful sound, like, "Hmm," and a comforting presence can help children focus. Assess whether children need a chance to cool off first before addressing the problem and if they do, give them ways to do that.

3) **Restate the problem**.
   Restate what they have told you about the difficulty and check back with them to see if you've stated it correctly. Help the children focus on the real issues at hand and not the resulting behavior. Stay objective yourself and avoid using language which makes judgements.

4) **Give choices**.
   Ask the children themselves if they can think of choices for what could happen next.

5) **Find a mutually agreeable solution**.
   Concentrate on what's positive and emphasize it. Congratulate the children for solving their problem.

The need for conflict resolution can emerge when you feel least ready and willing to engage with it, like hurrying for an outing, but when the process is tried, a dialogue lasting three or four minutes can be facilitated and prove helpful. [And can save a lot more than the time invested in some cases! Ed.]

For example, a family is on their way to a museum and two children are arguing about where they are going to sit in the car. The mother waits to see if they can come to an agreement and evaluates that they are at a stalemate because they are shouting at each other. She provides a calm framework to stop and think by turning around to face them. She says, "Let's talk about this." She states. "It looks like both of you want to sit in the same seat," and waits to see if she has articulated the problem. They nod. She asks each of them, "How could this be solved?" Each boy presents the same idea—he will get the coveted seat. When it is clear they need help reframing their options, she presents some process suggestions: the boy who has the seat both of them want could stay there on the way to the museum, and the other could have the seat on the way home. Or she could flip a coin. They decide to use a coin flip and abide by the result.

These five guidelines are not offered as a recipe but as a guideline to keep in mind. Sometimes you'll find that the problem is that each person in the conflict needs to have more information about what each person wants. During the third step, that of stating the problem, it's important to check if both people see the problem the same way. This is also a time when you might ask the disputants what each of them is feeling.

Part of developing our skill in assisting children is knowing when not to step in. For instance, three children were fighting over who had how many marbles. The young three-year-old who held most of the marbles was on the verge of being very upset. The teacher listened and noticed that a four-year-old whom the younger boy trusted was saying, "Oh, wait." Instead of stepping in, she watched the other children persuade the boy to open his hand and look at what he had. Together they divided the amount so that each of them had two marbles. They'd solved it themselves.

In a power struggle over an object sometimes the resolution is the realization that, "What you want to have happen can't happen right now." Then the adult can help the child think of his or her other choices: "You could choose to stay or you could go to the play house or the block area. What will you choose?"

In a situation of hitting, part of the problem is that the one who hit has accomplished what he or she wanted. Here, some helpful language can be: "Do you think she knows what you are angry about? Hitting doesn't tell her what you are angry about." Or, "Is there some other way you can tell her that you don't like to be tapped on the head besides hitting?"

When children are unwilling to engage in discussion of their actions, such as the child who has just hit another and now wants to run away, we explain while we hold their hands to keep them present, "The reason I'm holding you is because we still need to talk about it." We try to bring them into the circle of discussion so that they can experience that they will not be blamed or punished but will receive assistance.

Another familiar situation is that of tattling. Here, "What would you like to have happen?" is an important question to the child reporting. This way we let the child know that, not only the teacher, but they themselves can take action. We assist them in evaluating what they can do. Our language might include: "Why are you telling me this?" or "If that's bothering you, go back and tell him what you think," or "Why don't you go back and try to…" This way they see their own options in the matter.

In general we try to ask open-ended questions like, "Can you tell me why you are angry?" or " Can you think of another way to do this?" or "What do you need to be doing right now?" These help children focus upon their needs and help them be inventive in their solutions.

Descriptive statements can be employed to provide language for a situation and assist children in engaging with it.

Here are some sample descriptions:

• "Carmen and Alice are just getting to be friends. They may play with you later."

• "It's fun to do things for a long time. Maybe you could ask Gina how much longer she's going to swing."

• "He's still your friend and he likes you, he just wants to be alone right now."

• "It doesn't look like you are having much fun together. Would you rather choose separate places to play for a while?"

• "She sounds very angry with you. Can you tell me why she's so angry?"

Such statements help children gain understanding of a social situation, tell them that we have noticed their concern, and reveal their own choices.

Another interesting intervention is to offer opportunities to think about conflicts in a space of calm. At circle time at school we use puppets to act out conflicts that have occurred and ask the children, "What do you think they should do next?" This helps them expand their thinking about the options they have for their own behavior.

All in all, we try to consider ourselves as models so that we adults model the kinds of communication skills we are trying to encourage. We want children to feel that their needs can be expressed while they take responsibility for their actions and become aware of the needs of others.

We let children know that conflicts are a normal and healthy part of life, and they can meet them with confidence because they are resourceful people.

Peace Table

by Dolores J. Kirk

The Peace Table, a method of conflict management with young children, is one of many ways to take peace making from the abstract to the concrete. Problem-solving, compromising, and thinking through alternatives are learned skills. As teachers, we must find a way to give them the opportunity to experience the process, be responsible for their actions, and to be a part of the solution.

WHY: There is a need for children to learn problem-solving and alternatives to fighting in their lives, from the earliest age possible. Authoritarian methods keep all power, decisions, and enforcement in the hands of adults.

GOAL: To have children view the Peace Table as an opportunity for them to be heard and understood. If this method is used for punishment it cannot work. The most difficult aspect of the Peace Table process is relinquishing adult power. The Peace Table can become the most freeing experience that can happen for you as a teacher.

THE ONLY RULES: You must touch the table to talk, teachers, too! (Children love it when teachers must touch the table.) This gives control to the process. No one can come to the table and say what has already been said.

HOW:

- Any table or designated spot, e.g., rock, leaf, handkerchief, can be a Peace Table;

- Any place and any time;

- Teacher acts as the negotiator/moderator;

- Children involved in the conflict come to the Peace Table and tell what happened from their point of view; anyone in the class can add to the presenting of the problem;

- After the problem has been stated from all points of view, the children of the class are asked to give alternatives on how the problem could have been solved;

- The Teacher/Negotiator then needs to accept only real solutions or alternatives, e.g., child says, "They should be nice to each other." Teacher/Negotiator, "How could they do that?"

- Teacher/Negotiator restates the alternatives, but never declares which option they should take, or what to do; Teacher/Negotiator never asks them to say they are sorry, or forces adult solutions on them;

- Teacher/Negotiator asks the class to applaud themselves for being Peace Makers, and gives special Peace Maker stickers or badges to the offended.

TIME: Approximately ten minutes. Children have no problem listening or staying involved because they learn, after their first Peace Table, that full class participation is always allowed.

Some staff may object to stopping activities and calling the class together for a Peace Table because of schedules and time. To make peace a part of children's lives, you must be committed to the concept, and be willing to invest what is necessary for success.

NOTE: I have used the Peace Table and other methods of teaching peace in my classroom for five years. After the first of the school year, children call for Peace Table themselves. Many children have initiated the Peace Table in their homes, neighborhood play, and in their next school or class. The Peace Table cannot be done in isolation; every aspect of your classroom and your teaching approach needs to become a part of teaching peace, justice, and fairness, bringing shalom into children's lives in active, real ways.

Peace Week at Giving Tree School in Gill, Massachusetts

By Betsy Evans

In January we celebrate Peace Week at our nursery school, an occasion of our own invention. It coincides with Martin Luther King, Jr.'s birthday, and we have books about him as a peacemaker in our book corner. But most of all we focus upon the personal connections, and we encourage children to find their own identification with the concept of peace.

During the week, children draw pictures of their own peaceful places, we sing special songs, we read stories about cooperation and problem solving, and we think about what peaceful play is. The idea behind our approach to Peace Week is the concept of Key Learning Experiences developed by the High/Scope Foundation (600 N. River St., Ypsilanti, MI 48198). From the assumption that active learning is the heart of the developmental process, High/Scope had identified fifty key experiences to serve as guideposts for planning developmentally valid programs for young children.

We focus upon these two key experiences:

• Language: sharing meaningful experiences,

• Representation: sharing ideas through stories and drawings.

Here are some of the activities we did during Peace Week:

1) Recall: In our usual small group meetings after choice time we used these recall questions: What was something friendly you did during choice time? What is something you did that took two people to do?

2) Drawings of peaceful places: In small groups the book, *When Light Turns into Night* by Crescent Dragonwagon (Harper and Row, 1975) was read aloud about a girl who likes to go to the meadow behind her house by herself as night is beginning to fall. Children drew pictures of their own peaceful places, and then teachers wrote the words they dictated about their drawings: "This is me. I'm walking in the woods looking for a peaceful place in the winter." "I like playing in my green sandbox," Me sitting under my fir tree," "Trapezes are peaceful because it's quiet when you swing."

3) Collage: We made a multicultural collage of people of the world.

4) Creating a story: In small groups we began our group storytelling in the usual way by asking, "Who would you like to have be in the story?" But we added, "If there is a problem, the witch and monster will work to solve the problem." The children each held a piece of beeswax and warmed it while they participated. This is something we enjoy doing, and it helps them stay focused as they contribute and listen.

5) Songs: We sang and listened to songs that expressed concepts of peace. We made up new verses to "Down the Road" by Bill Staines to express what we'd like to see in the future, down the road. We sang, "The Sun Inside Us" by Sarah Pirtle ("The Wind is Telling Secrets," A Gentle Wind, 1988) that says, "We're so strong, we're so smart. We were born with the loving heart." We listened to the tape "Teaching Peace" by Red Grammer.

6) Peace Signs: We used round pieces of paper to make personal symbols of peace. This was possible because the children had a basis for symbolizing: the children create their own symbols in the fall and all their drawings, their cubbies, and other items are labeled with them.

7) Listing: We talked about things that made us feel peaceful. One child said, "Peace is my big bear, my medium bear, my little bear. They make me feel happy."
We also listed activities and kinds of peaceful play. The responses from one small

group included:
Peace is not walking into the house with muddy boots.
Peace is eating healthy stuff.
Peace is being silly.
Peace is not pulling hair.
Peace is sharing toys and something real tasty.

8) Reconceptualizing an aggressive animal: We read Tomie de Paola's book, *The Knight and the Dragon*, (Putnam, 1980) about a dragon and a knight who didn't really want to fight and end up starting a restaurant together using the dragon's firey breath for cooking. Afterwards children drew pictures of peace dragons.

We find that discussions about peace and cooperation reverberate long after Peace Week itself is over.

People Can Change: A Key Concept For Young People

By Sarah Pirtle

I took my son to our town library at the age of three. He spent a long time looking at the statue on the library lawn of a revolutionary war soldier with a musket. He asked with great interest, "Why does that man have a gun?"

I said, "That's a statue of a man who lived two hundred years ago in our town. That might have been a gun he used to hunt deer or birds to eat. But right then he was using that gun in a war. Sometimes when people had a problem they used guns and fighting to solve it. People are working to change now. When we have a problem we use words to talk about it."

People *are* changing. Never mind that I know that our country is spending half of its citizens' tax dollars on defense. I also know that skill at diplomacy is increasing exponentially, that elementary school children across the country are being trained as conflict managers, and colleges and universities are offering courses on conflict resolution. And I want him to know that, too. He lives in a world where people make changes.

Now my son is five. The theme that people can change has laced through at least four conversations in the past weeks. We celebrated Nelson Mandela's release from prison and talked about the way white people in South Africa are trying to change. In fact, we spent a long time looking at different pictures in newspapers just as we did when the Berlin Wall was opened.

In a different vein, we noticed that a local restaurant that only served sugary desserts now is also offering frozen yogurt without sugar. That means we now eat dessert there.

We talked about toy makers who make guns and how people are trying to get them to change and make different toys. We also talked about a child at nursery school who is learning to use words instead of pushing. People can change.

Here are five thoughts I offer on this process for both parents and teachers:

1) Think about the next step children are working on as they develop their social skills. Articulate this as a possibility for them. Give them language for what they are trying to do. For example, you might reflect back, "You said 'stop!' to Alex just now. I see you're using words when you are mad." Or, in another situation, "Friendly talking is one of the changes we're working on this year in our family." One phrase I have found helpful in letting children know of their options for self control is to say: "Can you stop yourself or do you need help stopping?" A child is throwing sand, for instance. You explain that other children might get sand in their eyes. The child keeps throwing sand. You can respond, neutrally, sincerely, "I'm concerned that this sand might get in other people's eyes. Can you stop yourself from throwing sand or do you need some help in stopping?" This clarifies that they have options for their behavior. Verbalizing the process helps bring to children's consciousness that they are developing the ability to control their impulses.

2) Reflect with them upon the changes they have made. For example, "You've really learned how to tell me when you need some help putting on your boots," in contrast to earlier behavior, maybe, of screaming or kicking to get help. "You've changed. You've found a way to ask for what you need." Or, "I've noticed you can do that farm puzzle now. Remember how it was difficult this summer? You've really grown."

3) Conceptualize every person as having the ability to change. Refrain from boxing in any adult or child into current behavior—whether it be a classmate who is hitting at school, or an elected official with whose views you disagree. So if a child is concerned about a friend's behavior, you can talk together about how he or she is working to change.

4)   Look for positive events in the world to call attention to, and speak about them as examples of people changing. For example, if there is an article about a shelter opening for homeless people locally, you can draw attention to it an discuss it together: "Look, people are finding a way to help those who don't have a place to sleep." Communicate the outlook that people are trying to find solutions to problems.

5)   Try using the theme of people changing as a framework that can interlace many different types of conversations.

My son still refers to the times when he was much younger and a particular friend often pulled his hair. Recently he let me know, "I think Casey has changed by now." From this, I gather that the theme of change is beginning to stick.

As he gets older I hope that this approach will give him a positive framework as he encounters the crises of world hunger, environmental degradation, war, and radioactive waste pollution. If he knows that people can change, that people can address problems and change them, he can, I hope, remember that despite the obstacles and critical conditions, this is not a terrible but a wonderful time to be alive. That is the foundation I want him to have.

Song "There Is Always Something You Can Do"

There Is Always Something You Can Do

Words and Music by Sarah Pirtle

1. There is al-ways some-thing you can do, do, do When you're
   al-ways some-thing you can do, do, do Yes, it's
   al-ways some-thing you can do, do, do When you're

get-ting in a stew, stew, stew; You can go out for a walk
dif-fi-cult but true, true, true. See it from each oth-ers' eyes,
get-ting in a stew, stew, stew. When you want to take a poke,

You can try to sit and talk. There's al-ways
Find a way to com-pro-mise. There's al-ways
Turn a-round and make a joke. There's al-ways

some-thing you can do. Wheth-er in a school or fam-'ly
some-thing you can do. You can use your smarts and not your
some-thing you can do.

ar-gu-ment, When you feel you'd real-ly like to throw a
fist, fist, fist; You can give that prob-lem a new twist, twist,

fit. Don't be trapp'd by fights and fists and an-gry threats,
twist. You can see it 'round a-bout and up-side down,

Reach out for this or-din-ar-y plan. 2. There is
Give your-self the time to find a way. 3. There is

Copyright ©1984 Sarah Pirtle. A Gentle Wind, publishers. Albany, N.Y. Used by permission.

The message of this song can be a useful tool to get children to "hear each other out" when anger and hurt feelings prevail; then to try for an agreement that seems fair to both sides. Children might also play-act such a scene.

GLOBAL AWARENESS

by Susan Hopkins

"Let there be peace on earth and let it begin with me." Song Title

Fear and lack of understanding of people different from ourselves is fundamental to the social and global problems we face today. We must provide rich educational experiences for our children so that they may learn of children from around the world.

When we learn of the differences and similarities among the peoples of the globe, we can begin to value the differences and connect via the similarities. When children learn to see beauty in people different from themselves and learn to value those differences, they begin to see the interconnectedness of all life on this planet. It is this fundamental principle of viewing all life forms on the earth as one interconnected life support system which will enable humanity to maintain the kind of spirit necessary to continue civilization as we know it.

Multicultural Education

The following statement has been taken from the National Association for the Education of Young Children "Position Statement on Developmentally Appropriate Practice in Early Childhood Programs Serving Children From Birth Through Age 8." (*Young Children*, September, 1986). It provides the rationale upon which to base multicultural curriculum. *Multicultural and nonsexist experience, materials, and equipment should be provided for children of all ages.* (Ramsey, 1979, 1980, 1982; Saracho & Spodek, 1983; Sprung, 1978).

Providing a wide variety of multicultural, nonstereotyping materials and activities helps ensure the individual appropriateness of the curriculum and also:

> 1 Enhances each child's self-concept and esteem;
>
> 2. Supports the integrity of the child's family;
>
> 3. Enhances the child's learning processes in both the home and the early childhood program by strengthening ties;
>
> 4. Extends experiences of children and their families to include knowledge of the ways of others, especially those who share the community; and
>
> 5. Enriches the lives of all participants with respectful acceptance and appreciation of differences and similarities among them.

Multicultural experiences should not be limited to a celebration of holidays and should include foods, music, families, shelter, and other aspects common to all cultures.

Looking at the NAEYC statement, two thoughts come to mind in terms of working on a daily basis with young children. First, we need to build upon the familiar since we are working with children who learn best when presented new concepts through their experiences. In working with multicultural concepts we will be most successful if we make good use of the children's own families as a starting place for learning. Secondly, we need to focus much attention upon countering stereotypes: cultural, social, gender, age, and disabilities to mention a few.

We are moving into an approach to multicultural education which integrates or "infuses" cultures into all aspects of the program. The feeling now is that the entire world is at our doorstep, in a way that it hasn't been before, and children must feel comfortable relating to people of all cultures. The emphasis is more toward stressing sameness than differences. We may talk about the various homes that people live in (condos, houseboats, pueblos, etc.), but we'll emphasize that all people need shelter and there are lots of fine ways to meet that need. We infuse cultures into our program first by involving our own families to share how they do things (housing, food, transportation, etc.) and then by setting up activities which relate. For example, children all share how they come to school and a graph is constructed of how many walk, ride the bus, come by car, etc. The discussion of these familiar transportation types then shifts to other types which are less familiar to the children. Activities are set up to help the children be aware of the concept that there are many appropriate ways to meet a need. While it is still fun to visit another culture, the main emphasis now is upon the infusion of cultures into our daily lives.

While infusing cultural activities into the curriculum, care must be taken to ensure that children understand that activities done by individual children may or may not be familiar to others who share the same ethnic or cultural background. Stereotyping is generalizing characteristics of individual members of any group to the whole group. As educators we need to be aware of activities that may be stereotypical. Wearing feathered headbands at Thanksgiving is an example that is most often found in curriculum resource guides and is most inappropriate as an activity to learn about current Native American culture. Any activities that misrepresent the members of a group should be examined in relationship to the "isms": racism, ageism, sexism, etc.

In one's efforts to counter stereotypes it is important that we help the children understand that each individual is unique and special. Yes, we all do belong to groups, and as members of groups we do have some similarities, However, what's really important is each person's uniqueness, and we must learn to know each individual person before thinking we know what he or she is like.

Although we have common needs for shelter, food, work, transportation, health care, and to be loved and needed, we may have very different ways of meeting these needs. Each person in this world has had unique experiences stemming from their family, where they live, who their friends are, to mention only a few influences. As a result, we must learn to appreciate the specialness of each person and try not to group all people together who may seem similar to us. In fact, that leads us right back to self-esteem—the development of high self-esteem is the very basis of our work!

Families

by Susan Hopkins

The family is the child's first group. The family has its own ways and customs, its value systems, its ways of meeting needs, and so on. It's the child's first community. The child experiences the world through the family. Therefore, it makes sense to start any study of people, community and cultures with the family—with the familiar. By getting information from the children's families about how they go about the basics of living, the children will feel proud of their own families and also see that their friends have ways of doing things that may be a bit different. A brief letter explaining that the children are learning about families and how they do things should give parents an introduction to this study. At that time it's fun to collect family snapshots to display in the classroom, too. Each week, or every few days, a different topic about family life can be explained. A note goes home to the family asking a question about one of the topics (see ideas following) and requesting a reply in the form of a snapshot, a note, or other appropriate concrete material. Questions could include:

—Who is in your family ?

—What kind of home does your family live in? Please send a photo or drawing.

—What kind of clothes does your family wear? Send picture.

—What kind of transportation does your family use?

—Please write a brief story about the work that is done in your family.

—What language do you speak at your house? If it is not English, could you send a tape recording of the language or visit our class?

—What kinds of foods does your family eat? Would you be willing to send a sampling of one of your child's favorites to school?

—How does your family have fun together?

—How do you celebrate holidays?

—Describe a custom or tradition in your family which is really important to you.

Families can respond to these questions in various ways from writing out a description or story, by pictures, by sending items to school, and possibly even by visiting. At school, wonderful use can be made of all this information by making displays of pictures, by having a tasting party, by letting children show their pictures or whatever they have brought, by making graphs to compare housing, transportation, work, etc. Most important, children need many opportunities to integrate all these different ways of doing things, so you'll want to set up dramatic play situations which involve different types of housing, transportation, work, and clothes. It's critical that the children actually experience doing things in a variety of ways so they'll be comfortable with "different." And being comfortable with differences means being able to cope in a world which is constantly changing. Our children must grow up feeling challenged and excited instead of fearing the new and different.

Cultural Appreciation Form

A follow-up to the study of families could involve a special emphasis on the cultural heritages within your group. A form follows which can be used to gain specific cultural information so that families can share their heritages with you. Once you've tallied the information you can plan ways to involve the families which range from integrating family cultural customs into your daily classroom setting to celebrating holidays. It's important to have the full range from common daily activities to celebrating holidays so that children will learn that other cultures are not simply celebrations. By incorporating utensils, clothing, language, music, etc. into your daily routines the children relate to cultures not as something "exotic," but simply as other ways to have their needs met. For example, we grownups have integrated eating spaghetti and lasagne into our "American" diets. We no longer think, "Let's eat something exotic like spaghetti…" It's fine we relate to more and more of these customs by integrating them into our daily lives. Celebrating holidays is great fun, but the daily business of living is what really matters.

Using the cultural information from families, we can learn about a variety of traditions from other cultures which follow a common theme such as "Breads Around the World." With an everyday need such as food, one has a starting point for learning about other cultures.

David Bedson
Age 7·10

Dear Parent: We value diversity of cultures and family traditions and encourage you to enrich our program with your customs. With parents' help it is our goal to foster an awareness and appreciation of the world community.

Your Name_____Child's Name _____

Principle Country(ies) of your family's heritage:

1.

2.

3.

4.

Please describe any family customs which are important to your family which would be helpful for us to be aware of at school.

Examples: Special foods your family eats.

Eating utensils.

Special clothing you wear.

Special daily routines (stemming from cultural background).

Special words or cultural terms your family uses. Is another language spoken in your home?

If yes,_____.

Which holidays specific to your cultural heritage does your family celebrate which you would like to have us to be aware of at school?

Name of Holiday   Date(s)

1.

2.

3.

4.

Would you be willing to help us learn more about your family's heritage by (check all which apply):

_____   1. Chatting with teachers informally about family customs/holidays, etc.

_____   2 Send some cultural materials to school for us to use in working with the children. Examples: music, stories, foods.

_____   3. Visit a classroom to assist the teachers in helping the children learn more about your culture.

People: Alike and Different Chart

People: Alike and Different
by Susan Hopkins

Concept	All people need to eat.	All people need shelter.	All people need clothes.	All people need transportation.	All people need to love and be loved.
Art Experience		Create different types of shelter from boxes and other materials.	Tie dye material or batik material.	Make picture book of transportation using cut up magazines, etc.	Paint on card using "Marble Painting" - put marble in paint and roll on paper.
Science Experience	Taste various breads: tortillas, crepes, biscuits, won tons.	Experiment with various types of weather to determine which type of house would give best shelter.	Continue experiment with weather to determine which clothes would be most comfortable.	Experiments with water and air.	
Music and Movement	"This is the way we bake our bread …"	Song: "The Colors of the Earth" — sung by Sarah Pirtle on The Wind is Telling Secrets		Movement to Music: Fast and Slow.	Musical hugs. Hugg-a-Planet.
Fine Muscle	Make bread - yeast bread involves kneading (see recipes).		Sewing and/or weaving.		Make a card for a friend, parent, or grandparent.
Large Muscle			Various types of clothes to try on.	Walk and run fast and slow.	
Language	Vocabulary: tortillas, won tons, crepes, pan, etc.	Vocabulary: hogans, igloos, grass huts, apartments, etc.	Which types of clothes are worn for various activities?	Vocabulary: trains, busses, cars, bikes, ships, airplanes, etc.	Dictate message for card telling why person is special.
Special Activities	Visit a bakery to see the different breads.	Pretend to set up housekeeping in the different types of homes.	Clothes from other cultures to see and try on.	Bring in a wheelchair for children to use.	Read On Mother's Lap by Ann Scott.

Introducing Young Children to the Globe

It may be helpful to introduce our world to the children using the following introduction to the globe by Dorothy W. Hewes, Ph.D., of San Diego State University:

Objective: To acquaint 4- or 5-year-old children with basic geographic awareness of the earth as a sphere and a globe as its representation.

Needed: Several models—a plastic or balsawood airplane, an antique car, a space station, or similar models (borrowed from older children, perhaps), and a large globe.

At circle time, show models one at a time. Lead discussion as to whether this is a "real" airplane, car, space station or whatever. "No, each is made to look like a real one, but what do we call things like this?" A child with a bigger brother usually says, "Models—my brother makes them." Talk a bit more about models. Then show the globe and in a conversational way talk about this being a model also. Some children already may know that the blue represents oceans, and may talk about where your center is located. "If we got in a car and drove all day, we'd get from here to here."

An appropriate accompanying song might be "It's a Small, Small World."

A follow-up activity might include putting small post–it tags on the globe to indicate where the families of children came from—parents will probably need to supply this information.

The globe should be kept available so that it can be referred to easily. For example, you might point out the origins of foods, stories, and music that are part of your curriculum. Use it as a weather map, indicating from where today's stormy or balmy weather blew in. By illuminating one side with a flashlight and leaving the opposite side in shadow, the reasons for day and night can be demonstrated.

You might also use your globe as the focus of special units, such as "Breads from around the world" or "Fruits from around the world." Be cautious about theme units that reflect stereotypes, such as "Children's clothes around the world," since most real children in today's world wear the same knitted shirts, sturdy pants, and skirts, and rubber soled shoes. How many of us were taught that Dutch children wore wooden shoes? In fact, classroom visitors from other parts of the country or the world usually look like the locals and by orienting children to where they have come from and what transportation they used, other lessons are learned.

Children should be able to touch their world model! There are stuffed cloth huggable globes and others that blow up like a beach ball. Most educational supply stores and catalogs of preschool curriculum materials now have appropriate globes for young children, which seems to indicate recognition of their value for teaching those underlying concepts needed for living together on that big blue ball which is home for us all.

"Passport" for Young Children

Paul Portner from Garden Grove, California uses "passports" in connection with global education. His passports are activity booklets for each child which include ideas such as learning some basic geography, making a family tree, learning to be helpful, practicing being a "peace person," and designing and sending a "peace card." Passports can be ordered from:
Paul Portner
Passport to Peace
13222 Lewis St.
Garden Grove, CA 92643

Passports and Pakistan

Abbie Enders, from Swarthmore, Pennsylvania, shares the following ideas which she used starting in 1953 upon her return from a year in Pakistan. In those days "multicultural education" was uncommon, yet Abbie writes, "My trip was so full of vital and lasting experiences and interesting people I felt I must bring some of this feeling and understanding of the world's people, especially Asian people, to my kindergarteners." Abbie goes on to describe the "trip" she and the children took around the world, visiting many different countries including Pakistan. To begin their adventure they packed their bags (literally) and then took a ride to the airport where they were allowed to experience actually getting on an airplane—not something most children had done in the early 1950's. In the course of their year-long travel experiences they learned a great deal of geography as they visited many countries on their way to Pakistan. Abbie made passports so the children could document their travels. "The passports had the child's picture in it, was signed by the child, had a picture of the flag of each country visited pasted in the passport along with the date of the visit. When the country was visited we had a mother or anyone who had lived in the country come and talk to the children, show pictures and tell them about the people, especially the children. We cooked a typical food and learned to count to five in the native language. Pictures, clothes, and utensils were available for the children's exploration. I was trying to have the children *feel* the different people of the world, their uniqueness, but also feel that we humans are one big family and feel much alike. We have interesting differences, but many more similarities."

Abbie also shared some of the ideas she and the children used especially to learn about Pakistan. In preparation she showed the children pictures of the people and the country and they had lots of discussions. They arranged the classroom setting to help the children feel as if they were really in Pakistan. Abbie modeled native dress and they cooked chapatis on a "ungaitie" (usually a clay stove, but Abbie's was made from a steel oil drum).

A recipe for chapatis can be found in the "Breads From Around the World" section of this book.

In addition to these activities, through friends in Pakistan they were able to find a "sister school" and set up exchanges of books by the children about "Our Day" as well as full-size body drawings of themselves. Such exchanges help children realize that children across the world have the same needs, although they may look very different.

In summary, Abbie comments "I think the experience of travel was very real for the children. They really felt the brotherhood of man."

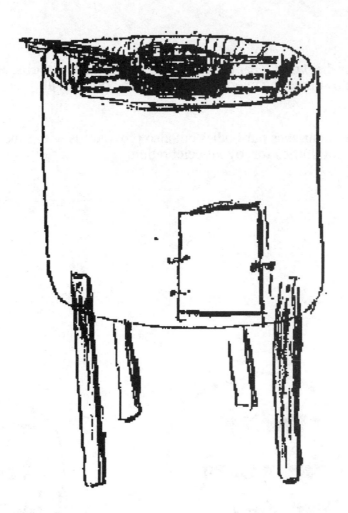

A Message from Pakistan, via the President

by Abbie C. Enders

K. Mohammed was a sixteen-year-old youth who worked for us in Pakistan. He understood English, and could converse readily in English, but could not read it. He asked me to teach him to read English, which I did. When George Bush was in Pakistan he was staying at one of their Great Houses for distinguished visitors. K. Mohammed was working at the Great House. He asked Mr. Bush, when he was back in the states, to get in touch with Mrs. Enders to thank her for teaching him to read, because he couldn't work at the Great House if he couldn't read English. George Bush, on returning to the United States, had his secretary telephone me. Then Mr. Bush telephoned himself, talking to me and to my husband, and personally delivered K. Mohammed's message. I think this speaks well for the character of George Bush that he would take this amount of trouble to follow the wishes of a young Pakistani working youth.

World Foods

People all over the world wear different clothes, do different jobs, and speak different languages. But we do something every day that is common to us all.

We eat!!

Eating together nourishes our bodies but also provides us with time to share feelings and information, opportunities for joyous celebration.

World Foods Chart

World Foods   by Kathy Olmstead

Concept	Everyone eats.	There are many foods around the world that are similar.	Children need roots and identity.	Spices come from all over the world and change the way things taste & smell.	People eat bread in many different forms.
Art Experience	Collage with food pictures cut out from magazines.		Make a bread basket with white playdough by weaving designs over bread pan—bake.	Make "spice circle". Children each share spice from home and glue on circle.	
Science Experience	Eat something from each basic food group. Discuss taste, smell, texture.	Make or buy and taste pancakes, tortillas, won tons, and crepes. Compare and discuss origin.	Taste many different kinds of breads from many ethnic sources.	Smell spice jars marked with pictures that represent home country (curry—India; chili—So. America).	Observe and compare making yeast & unleavened breads.
Music and Movement	Play games from Malvina Reynolds' album *Artichoke, Griddle Cake and Other Good Things*.		Play "Stir Fry." Tape very large circle on floor to be "pan." Children hop in a pan as they call out what food they are.		
Fine Muscle	Cut out pictures of people marketing, preparing, and eating a variety of foods.	Prepare and eat various cultured foods with appropriate utensils such as rice with chopsticks.		Push cloves into small styrofoam balls—hang together as mobile.	Stir, sift, knead, chop, etc.
Large Muscle	Walk to store and buy an item from each food group.				Act out adding ingredients for bread. Add yeast and everyone rises.
Language	Food Lotto. Make a set of cards representing many cultures.	Learn food names and associate with countries of origin.	Discuss kinds of food children eat at home—traditions from grandparents, etc.	Children share information about spice brought from home, how it is used in food, family traditions.	Learn bread names and associate with countries of origin.
Special Activities	Set up grocery store.		Have a "Festival of Breads." Parents bake bread & share culture and traditions.		Make various types of breads (see recipes).

<u>Breads From Around the World</u>

by Susan Knox

Most cultures have developed some form of bread. The theme, "Breads Around the World," can help children become aware of similarities in basic needs. By making a variety of different breads and learning a bit about the countries of origin, children will start to work with the concepts of same and different: we have the same basic needs but different cultures, we find different ways to meet the needs. Different can be exciting and wonderful!

Bread, Bread, Bread by Ann Morris shows photographs of children and bread from all around the world.

From India—Chapatis:

The breads that East Indians eat are very different from the plump, crusty loaves that are familiar to Westerners. Most East Indian bread has no leavening agent like yeast, so it does not rise when it is cooked. *Chapatis*, the most popular kind of East Indian bread, are flat pancakes that look something like Mexican tortillas. Like tortillas, they are cooked on a very hot, ungreased griddle.

2 1/2 cups whole wheat flour
2 Tbs. butter or margarine
1 tsp. salt
1 cup lukewarm water

1. Put 2 cups flour into a large mixing bowl.

2. Cut butter into small pieces. Make a hollow in the center of the flour and add butter. Rub butter into flour with your fingertips until mixture looks like large bread crumbs.

3. Mix salt into water. Add enough water, a little at a time, to flour mixture to make a firm (but not stiff) dough.

4. Knead dough in bowl for about 5 or 10 minutes. Cover bowl with a damp cloth and let stand at room temperature for at least 1 hour.

5. Divide dough into pieces about the size of walnuts, and roll each piece into a smooth ball with your hands.

6. Sprinkle remaining 1/2 cup flour onto a flat surface. With a rolling pin, roll out each ball until it resembles a thin pancake, about 1/8-inch thick.

7. Heat a heavy skillet or griddle over medium high heat. When the skillet is hot, place one chapati in the center. When small brown spots appear on the bottom and the edges begin to curl up (in about 1 minute), turn the chapati over with a spatula. Cook chapati for about 2 minutes or until small brown spots appear on bottom.

8. Continue cooking chapatis, one at a time. Wrap the cooked ones in a towel to keep them warm.

9. Brush cooked chapatis with butter and serve warm.

Makes 12 to 15 chapatis

From Hungary—Galuska:

Noodles and dumplings are popular additions to the good, hearty Hungarian soups and stews.

Galuska can also be served with main dishes such as paprika chicken.

2 Tbs. butter or margarine
1 egg
1 cup milk
2 tsp. salt
2 cups all-purpose flour
12 cups (3 quarts) water

1. In a medium bowl, cream 1 Tb. butter and stir in egg, milk, and 1 tsp. salt.

2. Add flour, a little at a time, stirring well after each addition, until mixture is the consistency of cookie dough. If dough is too stiff, add 1 to 2 Tbs. milk or water.

3. In a kettle, bring water and 1 tsp. salt to a boil over medium-high heat.

4. Dip a teaspoon in hot water, scoop up small pieces of dough (about 1/4 tsp. each), and drop carefully into boiling water. Dip spoon in hot water again if dough starts to stick.

5. Boil dumplings 2 to 3 minutes or until they rise to the surface. Drain in a colander.

6. Melt 1 Tb. butter in a medium saucepan. Add dumplings and stir gently until well coated. Serve immediately.

From Norway—Flatbread:

For some tasty variations of this recipe, try making flatbread using only white flour or only rye flour. You can also substitute 2/3 cup cornmeal for 2/3 cup flour.

1 1/3 cups stone-ground whole wheat flour
1 1/3 cups all purpose flour
1/4 cup vegetable oil
1 tsp. baking soda
1/2 tsp. salt
3/4 to 1 cup buttermilk

1. Combine first five ingredients in a bowl. Mix well.

2. Add only enough buttermilk to make a stiff dough.

3. Knead dough for 30 seconds on a well-floured surface (such as a board or tabletop).

4. Roll a medium-sized handful of dough (about 1/4 cup) into a ball and then pat it down into a flat circle. (Cover remaining dough so it doesn't become too dry.)

5. With a floured stockinet-covered rolling pin, and on a well-floured surface, roll dough into a very thin 10-inch circle. (If dough is sticking to the surface on which you are working, dust it with more flour.)

6. Place flatbread on an ungreased cookie sheet. (To make all of your flatbread pieces the same shape and size, score (mark with a deep line) dough circles with a knife, making triangles, squares or whatever shapes you prefer. After baking, break flatbread along scored lines.)

7. Bake at 350 degrees for 8 to 10 minutes. (Flatbread should be crisp and slightly brown around the edges) Cool on wire rack and repeat with remaining dough.

8. Break into pieces and serve plain or with desired topping, such as butter or cheese.

Makes 9 circles

From Great Britain—Rich Scones:

2 cups all-purpose flour
2 tsp. baking powder
1/2 tsp. salt
4 Tbs. lard
1/4 cup sugar
1/4 to 1/2 cup currants (if desired)
1/4 cup milk or buttermilk (enough to make a stiff dough)

1. In a large bowl, sift flour, baking powder, and salt.

2. Thoroughly mix in lard with your fingers. Then add sugar and currants. Mix well.

3. Stir in enough milk to form a stiff dough.

4. Preheat the oven to 425 degrees.

5. On a lightly floured surface (such as a board or tabletop), roll dough out until it is 3/4 inch thick, Cut into 2 inch circles (use a cookie cutter or the rim of a small drinking glass).

6. Place on a greased, floured cookie sheet and bake in the middle of the oven for about 10 minutes or until the tops are light golden.

7. Serve while still warm with butter, jam, and whipped cream, if you like.

Makes 12 to 16 scones

From France—French Bread:

This is a very simple, basic yeast bread recipe which works well with young children. They love to knead it, see it rise, and punch it down. It's really a special sensory experience!

1 pkg. dry yeast
1 Tb. soft shortening
2 Tbs. sugar
1 tsp. salt
3 1/2 cups flour
1 icy, beaten egg
Sesame seeds

1. Add 1 pkg. yeast to 1 1/4 cups warm water.

2. Mix in 1 Tb. soft shortening, 2 Tbs. sugar, 1 tsp. salt. Sift in approximately 3 1/2 cups flour gradually, until dough cleans bowl.

3. Knead 5 minutes on floured surface.

4. Let rise 45 minutes in well-greased bowl covered with towel in warm place.

5. Punch down, roll out on lightly floured board until dough is like a jelly roll.

6. Roll up in a loaf and place on a cookie sheet.

7. Make 3 to 4 slashes 1/4 way through bread; brush with icy, beaten egg.

8. Let rise 20 minutes.

9. Brush with icy beaten egg and sprinkle sesame seeds over top.

10. Bake at 375 degrees for 35-40 minutes.

Also see, from Ireland—Irish Soda Bread in the section on Ireland.

Desserts Around the World Chart

Desserts Around the World
by Nga Le and Susan Hopkins

Country	Wales	South America	Vietnam
	Favorite cookies in Wales are "Welsh Cakes."	South American people love to eat Dulce de Leche	Vietnamese children enjoy a dessert of Lychees and Mandarin Orange Jello.
Language	Welsh language: Cymru—Wales (not whales) Croeso - Welcome.	Spanish Language: table = mesa books = libros hand = mano good day = bueños dias	Vietnamese Language: see this book, page 65.
Foods	Roll and cut out "Welsh Cakes" (recipe follows).	Use spices in "raw" form such as nutmeg and vanilla bean. Make Jumañas—use yellow and green colors. Make Dulce de Leche (recipes follow).	Make Lychees and Mandarin Orange Jello (recipe follows).
Music and Dance	Favorite Welsh children's lullaby: "All Through the Night." Move bodies together to form a dragon.	South American music—dance & play instruments. Samba music.	
Clothes		Dye material green by mixing blue and yellow dyes. Weave with green and yellow dyed material.	Make Vietnamese hats—see unit on Asian culture for pattern.
Shelter			
Special Traditions	Celebrate St. David's Day on March 1st: Welsh Cakes, leeks, daffodils.	Carnival—celebration similar to Mardi Gras.	Celebrate Tet—similar to Chinese New Year.
Special Activities	Create a red Welsh dragon from boxes (see Asian curriculum). Compare pieces of coal and slate—both mined in Wales.		Fly kites—talk about air and wind. See unit on Asian culture for more ideas.

<u>Ethnic Recipes</u>

From South America—Indian Jumañas

South American Indians use achiote, the seed of the annatto tree, to color these tender nutmeg-flavored cookies yellow, and chop wild spinach for the green color. Food coloring is used for our version.

2/3 cup butter or margarine
1 cup sugar
2 eggs
1 tsp. vanilla
1/2 cup sour cream
2 3/4 cups flour
1 tsp. soda
1/2 tsp. salt
1/2 tsp nutmeg—grate from nutmeg "meat"
yellow and green food coloring
raisins or nuts

Heat oven to 375 degrees. Mix butter, sugar, eggs, and vanilla until fluffy. Stir in sour cream. Measure flour by sifting. Blend dry ingredients; stir into butter mixture. Divide dough into two portions; color half yellow and half green. Drop dough by heaping teaspoonsful on lightly greased baking sheet. Press raisins or nuts into center of each cookie. Bake 8 to 10 minutes, or until lightly browned. Makes 6 dozen cookies.

Dulce de Leche (Milk Pudding)

1 quart milk
2 cups sugar
1 tsp. vanilla extract
chopped nuts (optional)

In a heavy saucepan over high heat, bring the milk and sugar to a full boil. Immediately reduce heat to low, and cook; the mixture should bubble gently. Watch and stir occasionally.

When it takes on a caramel color and thickens to the consistency of caramel topping (2 or 3 hours) remove from heat and cool. Flavor with vanilla extract.

Place in freezer or refrigerator to chill. Chilling will thicken pudding. If you like, top with chopped nuts. Makes about 20 one tablespoon-size servings.

From Wales—Welsh Cakes
(Teisen Cymry)

by Nesta M. Isaac

From *Ninnau*, the North American Welsh newspaper.

2 cups flour
pinch of salt
2 tsp. baking powder
1/2 cup sugar
1/2 cup plus 1 Tb. shortening
1/2 cup currants (they can be purchased at your grocery store)
2 eggs well beaten with 2 Tbs. water or milk

Sift together flour, salt, sugar, and baking powder. Add shortening and rub into dry mixture. Add currants and mix well. Make well in center of mixture and wet down with liquid.

Roll out on floured board 1 to 3 inches thick and cut with round cookie cutter.

Bake on griddle until light golden brown on both sides. Do not overbake. (If taken off a little before completely done, cakes will finish while cooling on rack.)

Helpful Hint: Instead of rolling the dough out on a floured board and cutting it with a cookie cutter, try rolling the dough into a log with a 2-2 1/2" diameter for "slice and bake" type cakes. Dough freezes well in this form.

ALL THROUGH THE NIGHT

(Traditional Welsh Lullaby)

Sleep my child, and peace attend thee,

All through the night.

Guardian angels God will send thee,

All through the night.

Soft the drowsy hours are creeping,

Hill and vale in slumber sleeping.

I my loving vigil keeping,

All through the night.

Music can be found in: *The Great Songbook*, edited by Timothy John, published by Doubleday and Co., Inc., Garden City, N.Y. 1978.

See also *Rise Up Singing*, edited by Peter Blood-Patterson, for guitar chords and additional verses.

From Viet Nam—Lychees and Mandarin Orange Jello
by Nga Le

1 can lychees (11 oz.)
1 Tb. unflavored gelatin
1 can mandarin orange segments
1/4 cup lemon juice
1 tsp. vanilla extract
6 Tbs. granulated sugar

Drain the lychees (cut in half) and mandarin orange segments, reserving the syrup; add water to make 3 cups. Combine with sugar and gelatin and bring to boil, stirring occasionally, for 4 minutes.

Cool to room temperature. Stir the remaining ingredients into the cooled syrup. Chill 3 hours before serving. Makes 8 to 12 servings.

From Viet Nam—Sesame Lace Cookies

1/2 cup light corn syrup
6 Tbs. butter or margarine
1 cup all-purpose flour
1/2 cup granulated sugar
2/3 cup flaked coconut
1 Tb. sesame seeds
2 Tbs. sesame oil
3/4 tsp. vanilla extract

Combine corn syrup and butter in medium-sized saucepan. Stir over medium heat until butter melts; remove from heat. Add remaining ingredients; mix well. Drop by level teaspoons onto lightly oiled foil-lined baking sheet, at least 3 inches apart. Bake in 350° F. oven, 12 to 15 minutes, or until golden brown. Cool 5 minutes, or until cookies peel away easily from foil. Store in airtight container. Makes about 3 1/2 dozen cookies.

CÁM ƠN (Thank You)

CHÚC MỪNG NĂM MỚI
(Happy New Year)

VIỆT NAM (Viet Nam)

Specific Culture Studies

At times you may want to focus strongly on a particular culture; perhaps you have a population at your school which warrants special emphasis on an area of our world.

Following are several activity charts for various cultures. They are samples only and can be adapted as appropriate. In addition, we encourage you to research the countries which you enjoy learning about, or in which you have some personal interest, creating your own ideas. If you are enthusiastic, the children will pick up on your excitement and will share in your delight in learning about other people.

As you plan your multicultural curriculum it is most important to work with various cultures in such a way that the children integrate the values and traditions of those cultures into their own framework of the world. We don't want to give the children a "tourist" approach to learning about the world community by simply doing a few crafts and eating some ethnic foods. Instead, we need to become more deeply involved by delving into important cultural traditions and value systems. For example, learning about the people of Wales would be superficial unless we did a great deal with singing because the Welsh people value singing as being their way to communicate with God. We can note the special connection Native Americans have with their environment. We can work with the children to understand that we must take care of our land, water, and air—concepts relating to pollution are important to work on with young children, and can be carried forth through clean up time, litter gathering walks, conservation of water, and so on.

The danger of doing specific culture studies with young children is that they may generalize and think in stereotypes, i.e. all Asian people eat with chopsticks, or Welsh people sing all the time. In order to prevent stereotypes-thinking from developing it is important to continue to integrate the cultural experiences into your daily classroom long after the study is finished. Keep the chopsticks, along with other eating utensils in the dramatic play corner so all children can use them. Use lots of music from many cultures in your program. Eat foods from all over the world at meal and snack times. Go back and enjoy the experiences time and again and incorporate them into daily living.

Native American

by Janey Marquez

One child in my class of three-and-one-half to four-year-olds solemnly announced that there are no Indians where he lives. When questioned as to what he meant, he repeated, "There are no Indians where I live." When asked "Where do you mean?" he said, "Santa Ana." When assured that there most certainly were Indians living in Santa Ana, he replied "Well, they don't live on Baker Street."

He was sure that there were no Indians there because his mental image was of Indians in regalia, and since he'd seen none, they weren't there. Later on, when a friend who is Native American visited our classroom, one of the children told Diane that we had an Indian in our class, but "This one was a good Indian because she didn't have a bow and arrow." Another child kept calling her "Indian," as if this were her name, as if she were an object, until we went around our circle and introduced everyone and they each greeted "Suzanne." Could it be that the "I is for Indian" in so many of our books innocently translates into the impersonalization of Indians to some young children?

Children derive their knowledge of the "Indian" from a media that continues to depict Indians as savage, wild and uncontrollable, as viewed in several current television commercials.

The traditional beliefs of the first inhabitants of this country were to use the resources of our land with care and respect. This is reflected in the beliefs of many of the tribes throughout the country. Those of us working with young children on issues of peaceful education, sharing, cooperation, and protection of our planet can do well to learn and include many of these ideas in our day-to-day journey through our lives and into the future. Native American studies should be included in all curricula. All too often, the only time during the year that we include our first inhabitants in the class calendar is during Thanksgiving, and then often in a manner that inaccurately and inappropriately depicts the "Indians" as an episode in the past of American history.

Every region in the United States has a history and a culture that preceded the advance of European occupation. To maintain a curriculum that considers young children's learning style and accurately represents native cultures, it might be best to study local history and use it as a starting point to introduce the Native American perspective into the curriculum. (To find out more about tribes in your area, contact your local Indian Center or write the Bureau of Indian Affairs, Dept. of the Interior, Washington D.C. 20240.)

Another approach could be to take several aspects that are a common thread in many native cultures, e.g., music, corn, respect for the environment, and study them.

It is imperative that young children learn accurate knowledge of Native American culture and respect for their beliefs and lifestyles. We, as adults, must often unlearn what we have been taught as well as rethink our understanding of history, perhaps relearning, and thus adjusting our teaching practices to provide and educate for a better understanding in the future. When we present Native American culture to young children, as with any other culture, we must try to use materials that present accurate and positive portrayals of the members of the cultural groups we are learning about.

When in doubt about a given material, it is probably better not to use it. Many curricula on the market today still include suggestions for activities that are offensive to members of the ethnic group being studied.

Many resources provide reviews and guidelines of materials. One of the best is the Council for Interracial Books for Children, 1841 Broadway, New York, N.Y. 10017.

Native Americans Chart

Native Americans   by Janey Marquez

Concept	Native Americans live in houses, dress, and work as we do.	Native Americans introduced us to many varieties of foods and plants.	Native Americans share a long heritage of art and music.	Native Americans have a reverence for nature.	We share and learn from Native Americans.
Art Experience		Cut out pictures of types of foods used by Native Americans.	Explore various media used by Native Americans: clay, paints, sand painting.	Collect natural material for collage.	Stencils of Native American designs.
Science Experience	Look at materials used in buildings.	Identify foods cultivated by Native Americans: corn, squash, chilis, etc.		Discuss animals important to Native Americans.	
Music and Movement		Make a musical instrument from a gourd and seeds.	Use a variety of music from tribal songs by Native American artists.	Pretend to be or find animal "brothers."	Make and use drums or rattles for group time.
Fine Muscle		Make baskets, weave a placemat.		String bead necklaces, use natural materials.	Use stencils of Native American designs to do tracing and outlining.
Large Muscle	Build a rush house or make adobe.		Run relay races, hoop races, tag.		
Language	Use pictures and books to explore types of housing.		Read Native American poetry, stories.	Flannel board stories from animals.	
Special Activities	Have a guest come to school to tell about work.		Visit a powwow or invite dancer to school.		

Corn Chart

Corn Unit
by Janey Marquez

Concept	We eat products from corn such as popcorn.	We use corn today.	We used corn in the past.	Other cultures use corn.	Corn grows.
Art Experience	Glue popcorn kernels on ears of corn shape.			Use corn cobs as brushes for paining.	
Science Experience	Make popcorn, discuss changes (sensory).	Make cornbread.	Grind corn, using grinding stone.	Use corn tortillas for snacks.	Plant corn.
Music and Movement	"Popcorn" on *We All Live Together* volume II.			Corn dance as done by the Pueblo Indians.	"Seed Song" from *Windows* by Tom Hunter.
Fine Muscle	Glue popcorn.	Make corn husk dolls.		Take corn kernels off cob.	
Large Muscle	Pretend to be popcorn.		Grind corn.		
Language	Book *Popcorn* by Tomic de Paola.	Identify various corn products.	Stories of development of corn such as… →	*Corn is Maize* Aliki.	Flannel board story, how corn grows.
Special Activities				Visit a tortilleria if available.	Visit a farmer's field or family garden.

Hopi Indian Culture

by Susan Hopkins

Hopi Patterns

Kachinas—Dolls which are spirit-personifications relating to important aspects of Hopi life
   such as religion, rituals, seasons, clans, etc.

Hopi Sun Kachina taken from: *Indian Designs* by David and Jean Villaseñor.
Naturegraph Publishers, Happy Camp, CA. Used by permission.

<u>Silverwork</u>—Hopi overlay—a collage could simulate the overlay techniques by glueing paper on top of paper in designs.

<u>Pottery</u>—Coil method using red/brown clay and painting designs on the pot after it dries.

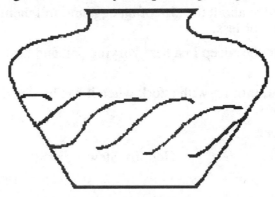

Hopi Weaving

Hopi weaving is traditionally done by the men using cotton. Teachers and children together can make long red waist sashes from material such as burlap. The ends can be fringed and knotted. White thread can be woven into the burlap in diamond shapes. Green thread can be woven into borders. The sashes are usually about five inches in width. Other weavings with yarn or paper can be used for placemats, wall hangings, etc.

<u>Hopi Recipes</u>

The following four recipes are taken from *Hopi Cookery* by Juanita Tiger Kavena, University of Arizona Press, Tucson, 1987.

Hopi Fry Bread (Wequivi)

(Serves six to eight)

4 cups white all-purpose flour
5 tsp. baking powder
1-1/2 tsp. salt
2 to 2-1/4 cups water
shortening, as needed

1. Mix flour, baking powder, and salt in a large bowl.

2. Gradually stir in water to make a soft dough.

3. Continue stirring until dough is smooth and shiny.

4. Cover bowl with a clean towel and set aside for thirty minutes.

5. Shape dough into 16 balls, about the size of an egg, and roll them on a lightly floured board to 1/2-inch thickness or less.

6. Pour shortening 1 1/2 inches deep in a heavy frying pan and heat until it is just before the smoking point.

7. Place dough into hot fat, turning with a fork when it has browned on one side until it is golden brown on both sides.

8. Drain on absorbent paper.

Hominy Stew

(Serves ten)

2 pounds mutton or beef backbones, cut into 1-inch serving sizes
water
10 cups hominy (fresh, dried, or frozen)
1 Tb. salt

1. Put meat in a large pot, cover with water, and stir in salt.

2. Cover pot and simmer meat for about one hour, and then add hominy.

3. Continue cooking, in covered pot, until hominy becomes soft, usually overnight.

Fresh Corn Chile Fritters

3 cups fresh corn, scraped from the cob
1/4 cup chopped fresh chile
1 tsp. salt
1 egg
shortening

1. Grind corn very fine with a hand meat grinder.

2. Add chile and salt to corn.

3. Mix in egg.

4. Cook on a greased griddle, as you would pancakes.

This dish can also be baked in a casserole, in a 350°F oven for thirty minutes, or until set. Fritters are served as a main dish or with plain meat stews.

Hopi Pinto Beans

2 1/2 cups dried pinto beans
7 cups water
1 cup bacon or a piece of ham
salt to taste

1. Wash and sort beans carefully.

2. Put beans in a bean pot or large saucepan and add bacon or ham and 7 cups of water.

3. Simmer for three hours or until beans are tender, stirring occasionally and adding hot water as needed.

4. Add salt to taste. (The amount will vary according to the quantity of salt in the meat and individual preference.)

5. Serve as a main meal with tortillas and a green vegetable, or as a light meal with fried bread.

Traditional Hopi Culture Chart

Traditional Hopi Culture
by Susan Hopkins

Concept	Hopi people grow crops such as squash, beans, corn, cotton. They also herd sheep.	The Hopi eat special foods such as fry bread, piki bread, mutton stew.	The Hopi live in "apartment-type" homes called pueblos.	Hopi crafts include silver work, weaving, pottery.	Hopi people carve Kachina dolls to represent spirits.
Art Experience	Collage of seeds, wool, & cotton to represent Hopi crops.		Create pueblos from boxes—paint and decorate with symbols.	See patterns for "silver work," weaving, pottery.	Make paper Kachina dolls—decorate with feathers.
Science Experience	Grow Hopi foods in a garden, take care of them and harvest.	Experience changes in materials as foods are prepared.		Samples of raw silver, cotton, wool, and clay. Discuss where they come from.	Demonstrate a little wood carving.
Music and Movement	Creative movement for seeds growing and being harvested.				Hopi music and dance. Folkways recordings.
Fine Muscle		Grind blue corn meal. Use in corn muffins.	Decorate homes with pictures, etc.	Crafts all involve fine muscle work.	With teacher's help, practice carving some soft wood.
Large Muscle	Gardening—hoe, weed, water.		Paint the outside of the pueblos.	Corn cob darts made with feathers on ends. Throw through circle made of corn husks.	
Language	Vocabulary: cotton, wool, beans, squash, corn.	Vocabulary: piki bread, blue corn meal, mutton stew, etc.	Vocabulary: pueblo, village.	Picture symbols to be used in silver work, weaving, and pottery.	Vocabulary: ceremony, carving, Kachina dolls.
Special Activities	Have a dinner using foods you have grown, harvested, and prepared in the Hopi way.	Prepare Hopi foods; see recipes.	Dramatic play in the pueblo.	Use the crafts in a ceremony involving music and dancing, foods, ceremonial clothes such as silver and woven sashes.	

Martin Luther King, Jr. Day, Celebrating African-American History

by Susan Hopkins

Following are some ideas for working through a few concepts relating to the history of the African-American people as they've strived to be treated fairly. These concepts of peace and justice are ones which children can begin to relate to in concrete ways. Most importantly, they are basic concepts of peace and justice which all people must develop if we are to live together as a world community.

Young children always love a birthday party, so why not celebrate Martin Luther King's birthday with a party in January? We celebrate Dr. King's birthday because he taught us to live peacefully. Instead of fighting to get what we want, he taught us to use our words. He taught us to tell people what we need. Adults and children could take turns doing role plays to act out getting needs met in peaceful ways. Situations could involve typical problems young children encounter such as wanting a turn, being called an unkind name, or being left out of a game.

Martin Luther King, Jr. also taught us about treating all people fairly. One idea to help children grasp this concept could involve the use of various colored (purple, white, pink, green, brown, etc.) paper dolls. All the dolls who are purple must sit in the back of the classroom where they can't see the story book that the teacher is reading very well. How do they feel? Would you like to be treated that way? Martin Luther King said it is not fair to make some people sit in the back if they don't want to. An extension of this concept could involve creating classroom rules as a group which would be fair to everyone.

Children enjoy going one step further with the concept of fairness and learning the Rosa Parks story. They like to hear the story told about how she refused to sit in the back of the bus just because the rule said that people with brown skin had to sit there. Because she refused to obey the rule, she went to jail. Then lots of people wouldn't ride the busses anymore until the rule was changed. The children enjoy seeing pictures of Rosa Parks and they love learning the song, "We Shall Overcome". Most specially, they really integrate these ideas and the history when involved in acting out the story. They love to refuse to sit in the back of the bus just like Rosa Parks. It's important to talk about the feelings involved. A word of caution: since jails can be very scary to children that part of the story should be simplified so those feelings won't dominate. Also, children sometimes don't understand why a good person goes to jail, but they do grasp sticking up for something to make it fair for all involved.

The concepts of peace and justice, of nonviolence and fairness, must be emphasized and worked through constantly throughout the year. Dr. King's birthday (January 15th) is an important time to talk about them, and role play. If we are willing to work untiringly on them every day, all year long, we will accomplish a more peaceful world.

African-American History

by Janey Marquez

After Martin Luther King, Jr. Day in January and Black History Month in February, many of us may wonder how we can continue to incorporate aspects of African-American history and culture into our curriculum the rest of the year. The following plans offer some ideas.

While it is important to recognize and celebrate these special dates, it is not enough to recognize African-American culture, or any other culture for that matter, only on those special occasions. At the same time, it is important that activities be presented in a way that enables children to build new learning into already acquired skills and knowledge, and to have a framework for providing them with experiences which are meaningful and appropriate for their developmental level. This means that experiences should be concrete, hands-on, and interactive. Often when we talk about cultures, we are talking about abstract concepts that are very difficult for children to grasp.

Building up a variety of experiences for children that gives them an opportunity to explore aspects of other cultures while building onto experiences they already have, is the most effective way to learn.

Obviously, first-hand experience with children and adults from other cultures is the best, but children can also learn about cultures with which they do not have direct contact. In addition to any specific curriculum about African-Americans and their African heritage, there should be materials in the classroom that reflect the culture. There should be a variety of dolls, including different types of African dolls, combs for Afro-type hairstyles, books that reflect African-American children and their families, and folklore records from popular recording artists as well as ethnic music, plus experience with foods associated with African-American culture during snack or lunch programs. These types of materials should be available at all times.

Jessica, age 4, Rm.

A black person going on the front of the bus.

Freedom Songs

WE SHALL OVERCOME

We shall overcome, we shall overcome,
We shall overcome, someday.
Oh, deep in my heart, I do believe,
We shall overcome someday.

We are not afraid, we are not afraid,
We are not afraid today.
Oh, deep in my heart, I do believe,
We shall overcome someday.

We are not alone, we are not alone,
We are not alone today.
Oh, deep in my heart, I do believe,
We are not alone today.

Verse 4: The truth will make us free

Verse 5: We'll walk hand in hand

Verse 6: The Lord will see us through

Verse 7: Black and White together (now)

Verse 8: We shall all be free

(The third and fourth lines of all the verses will be the same as the third and fourth lines of verse 1.)

"We Shall Overcome" by Zilphia Horton, Frank Hamilton, Guy Carawan & Pete Seeger. TRO—© Copyright 1960 (renewed) and 1963 by Ludlow Music, Inc., New York, NY. Used by permission, all rights reserved.

Music can be found in: *Best Loved Songs of the American People*, p. 374, Denes Agay, 1975, Doubleday and Co., Inc., Garden City, N. Y.

WE SHALL NOT BE MOVED

(Black Spiritual)

Chorus:

We shall not, we shall not be moved;
We shall not, we shall not be moved;
Just like a tree, planted by the water,
We shall not be moved.

Verse:

We are fighting for our freedom,
We shall not be moved;
We are fighting for our freedom,
We shall not be moved.
Just like a tree planted by the water,
We shall not be moved.

See *Rise Up Singing*, by Peter Blood-Patterson, A Sing Out publication, for additional freedom songs and more verses to those listed above.

Kwanzaa

by Viann Sanders

A special celebration for African-Americans is Kwanzaa. Translated from Swahili, Kwanzaa means "first fruit." The concept comes from the festivities that occur at the time of harvesting the first fruits of the year in Africa. The theme for Kwanzaa centers around seven principles: unity, self-determination, working together, sharing, purpose, creativity, and faith. The celebration lasts from December 26th to January 1st.

For African-American families, Kwanzaa is a time for being together and expressing pride in their heritage. To celebrate Kwanzaa, people may exchange gifts, visit each other, and serve traditional African feasts. A special area is set up that includes a unity cup and a candleholder for seven candles. The colors red, green, and black symbolize Kwanzaa and are used in decorations.

Since unity is so important to this occasion, different types of unity could be discussed. Some suggestions are the family, a neighborhood, people doing similar things, a country, or an ethnic group. Other activities that can be included while learning about African heritage are music, dancing, singing, and food (bananas, nuts, and sweet potatoes).

Kwanzaa Recipes

Sweet Potato Pie

1 frozen 9-inch pie crust (or one you prepare yourself)
    2 cups cooked sweet potatoes
    1 sliced banana
    1/4 cup unsweetened frozen apple juice concentrate
    1/3 cup orange juice
    2 eggs
    1 tsp. cinnamon

1. Blend filling ingredients well.

2. Pour into the pie shell.

3. Bake at 400 degrees for 40 minutes.

Makes 12 small servings.

Nutty Bananas

1. Mix finely chopped or grated peanuts with wheat germ and spice to taste with cinnamon.

2. Place small amounts of the mixture on paper plates and give each child one half of an unpeeled banana.

3. Let the children peel their own bananas and dip them into the nut mixture before taking each bite.

African-American History and Culture Chart

African-American History and Culture
by Janey Marquez

Concept	People from many cultures participate in similar daily activities.	People of all races are proud and beautiful.	People from all cultures make important contributions to society.	People from all cultures grow and use special foods.	In all countries people tell folk tales and share about their cultures.
Art Experience	Wood block stamp painting.				Make masks of collage or tissue paper.
Science Experience	Plant squash or gourd plants—cultivate.	Discuss skin colors, mixing paint.	Stop Light—by Doris Sims, about Garret Morgan (activities and discussion of stop light).	Prepare greens.	Make rattles and drums.
Music and Movement	Call and Response songs i.e.: "Miss Mary Mack;" "Did You Feed My Cow?"	"If You Miss Me at the Back of the Bus" song.	Jazz and Dixie Land Ella Jenkins Play Your Instruments (album).	Chants for growing or preparing food.	Play African rhythms—move to the music.
Fine Muscle	Make bead necklaces, fill shakers.	Try braiding doll's hair.	Work on masks, brush paint.	Dice food for preparation.	Fill rattles with beans or gravel.
Large Muscle			Dance to various music; popular, jazz, Africa, reggae.	Work in garden, plant seeds, weed, tend.	Act out Anansi's sons' adventures.
Language	Moja means One Jambo means Hello by M. Feelings.	Talk about Rosa Parks, Martin Luther King, Jr.	Learn names of music, African instruments.	Discuss foods.	Read Anansi the Spider by Gerald McDermott.
Special Activities		Read Cornrows, by Camille Yarbrough. Talk about hair styles.		Visit a "Soul Food" restaurant.	

Asian Culture Curriculum

by Susan Hopkins

The following concepts and activities relating to Asian culture may be used most effectively when incorporated into the early childhood curriculum on a regular basis. You may want to specifically emphasize Asian culture during one time period, but it is important to continue your involvement with the culture by repeating activities, by leaving picture displays up, by remembering thorough discussions and comparisons, and carrying certain activities (such as silkworms) on for a long period of time. Asian culture doesn't happen only at Chinese New Year!

Theme: Asian Culture

Concepts:

Asia is a part of our world. Some countries in Asia include China, Japan, Korea, Vietnam, and Thailand. People everywhere in the world have the same basic needs for food, clothes, shelter, communication, recreation, and expressing feelings. However, different cultures have created different ways of meeting these needs. By studying other cultures we can learn to respect and appreciate the differences and similarities.

Curriculum Ideas:

Craft Activities

1. Origami—Japanese paper folding.

2. Chinese dragon made from cartons and boxes—paint boxes, connect with string, and let the children wear the boxes on their heads for a parade. Careful adult supervision is needed as the children can't see through the boxes. See pattern for dragon head.

3. Blow Paintings—use straws, powder paint, and paper. Dip straw into paint, let a drop of paint fall onto paper, then blow through the straw to push paint in wiggly lines. Printing with sponges on other material can add another dimension to the artwork.

4. Fish Kites—see pattern included. Materials needed include wrapping paper, pipe cleaners, model glue, cut out eyes and string.

5. Oriental Lanterns—see pattern included. On one day paint the lanterns using soft colors of water color paints. The next day cut the lanterns on the lines as pattern shows and staple together. Add a handle. These can be hung up around the room to add to the feeling of Asian culture.

6. Vietnamese Farm Hats—see pattern included.

7. Crepe Paper Prints on Fish—pattern included. Cut fish shape from crepe paper, brightly colored. Place cut out fish on manilla paper or newsprint and paint it with vinegar water (1/2 vinegar, 1/2 water). When the paper is dry, peel off the crepe paper fish and see the print underneath.

Cooking

1. Tea Eggs—Boil one egg per child for 10 minutes, cool in water. Crack the shell with a spoon. Combine 3 tablespoons of black tea, 2 tablespoons of salt, and 2 tablespoons of soy sauce; add to the water. Boil eggs in the tea mixture for 20 minutes. Remove shells to discover a pretty pattern.

2. Meat-filled Won Tons—for 12 children.
   12 Tablespoons raw hamburger
   6 Teaspoons Soy Sauce   Mix together.

   Each child chop up 3 bean sprouts and add to the mixture. Each child add a pinch of minced green onion. Put 1 teaspoon of the hamburger mixture in the center of a won ton skin and fold in half to form a triangle. Dampen the edges to make them adhere to each other. Won tons may be deep fat fried for 1 to 2 minutes or simmered gently in chicken soup.

3. Butterfly Won Tons—take a won ton skin and cut a T-shaped slit in the middle. Draw two corners through the slit so that the won ton resembles a butterfly. Fry in oil until crisp, drain, and sprinkle with powdered sugar.

4. Sushi—use Japanese molds or form into balls with hands.

   Combine:
   > 2 cups cooked rice
   > 1/4 cup sugar
   > 1 cup grated carrot
   > 1/3 cup vinegar
   > 3/4 tsp. salt

   Boil vinegar and salt together briefly, then add rice and carrot. Form into balls.

   Japanese children often eat these for their lunches.

5. Egg Foo Yung—Grow your own mung bean sprouts and then use them in this dish. Each child cracks one egg into bowl and beats it. Add a pinch each of tuna, shrimp, chopped celery, bean sprouts, chopped green onion and stir. Pour into frying pan and fry as a pancake. Season with soy sauce and eat.

Science

1. Grow Mung Beans—Children grow their own in baby food jars by covering several seeds with warm water and soaking overnight in a dark place. Then drain and rinse at least twice daily for 4 or 5 days. When sprouted they are ready to use in Egg Foo Yung.

2. Silkworms—Silkworm eggs can often be requested from school districts or local colleges. They hatch when mulberry trees leaf out and then must feed on the mulberry leaves constantly until they spin their cocoons. The children take much interest in feeding them, watching them grow and change. Charts showing changes can be developed with the children.

3. Carp Fish—using photographs of fish help the children compare the looks and uses of carp and other kinds of fish. Charts of comparisons may be developed.

Stories

1. Matsuno, Masako, *A Pair of Red Clogs*, The World Publishing Co., New York.

2. Mosel, Arlene, *The Funny Little Woman*, E. P. Dutton, New York, 1977.

3. Mosel, Arlene, *Tikki, Tikki, Tembo*, Scholastic Book Services, New York, 1968.

4. Wyndham, Robert, *Chinese Mother Goose Rhymes*, The World Publishing Co., New York, 1968.

Dramatics

1. Using clothes from various Asian countries, try them on, compare how they look and feel, and use them in role playing, how families live in Asia.

2. Lower tables (remove legs if necessary) so that children sit on mats on the floor to eat their meals.

3. Use chopsticks for eating.

4. Japanese Tea Ceremony—all remove shoes and sit on the floor for the ceremony.

Movement Exploration & Music

1. Dragon walk—move like a dragon. Create different ways of moving.

2. Use Ann Barlin's "Shojojo" song for moving like a badger (from the Berman/Barlin record, see reference in Additional Resources for Children).

3. Any music from Asian culture can be listened to as background music. Children may also enjoy simply moving to it and/or playing rhythm instruments along with it.

4. Scarves can be used by children as they move to music.

Cognitive Games

1. Using chopsticks, sort fluffy colored yarn balls by color into bowls.

2. Pick-up sticks.

Language

1. Learning a few words in another language is fun for the children and it helps them relate to a different culture.

2. Discussion of the many important concepts, with much opportunity for the children to express their thoughts is important.

3. Language experience stories can be created about the various activities in the classroom.

Special Events: It is very important to include any families of Asian background in the study. These families can contribute ideas and materials and bring a richness to the group in very special ways. And, of course, their children feel great pride in their heritage. Do invite them to contribute.

Asian Cultures Chart

Asian Cultures — by Susan Hopkins

Concept	Children in every country enjoy making and playing with toys.	Throughout the world people grow plants and use them in special foods.	People everywhere have special ceremonies & traditions for their holidays.	People have learned how to make clothes for themselves in many different ways.	In all countries people tell folktales about their culture.
Art Experience	Fish kites.		Create a Chinese Box Dragon.		Collage rice on cut out circles.
Science Experience	Air experiments.	Sprout mung beans.		Observe & chart silkworms' growth.	Cook rice. Talk about how rice is grown.
Music and Movement		Pretend to be a mung bean seed that sprouts.	Dragon walk.	Act out the concept of metamorphosis.	Act out the story: *The Funny Little Woman.*
Fine Muscle	Cut and glue the kite.	Measure, stir etc., in cooking.	Paint the dragon.	Hold silkworms gently.	Make rice balls.
Large Muscle	Flying the kite.		Dragon parade.	Asian clothes to use for dress-up.	
Language	Discussion of air concepts.	Write story emphasizing sprouting & cooking.	Experience story about dragons.	Discuss & display silk garments.	Read: *The Funny Little Woman* by Mosel.
Special Activities		Cook Egg Foo Yung with own sprouts.		Silkworms - observe process of metamorphosis.	

Box Dragon

Cut box mouth
along dotted line
for mouth
opening.

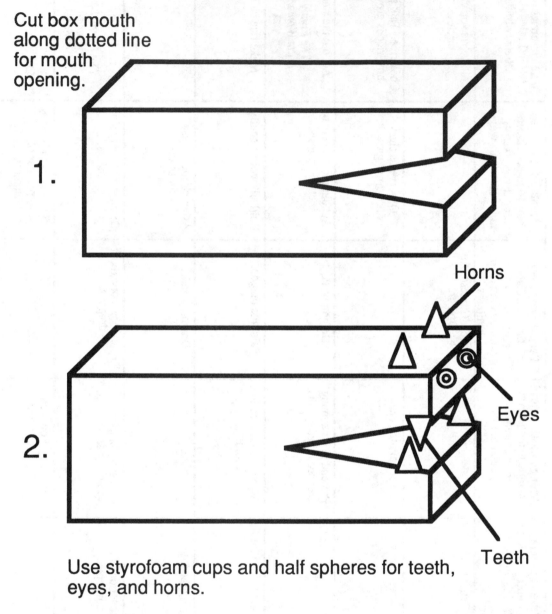

1.

Horns

Eyes

2.

Teeth

Use styrofoam cups and half spheres for teeth,
eyes, and horns.

3. Paint head and boxes of various sizes

4. String together boxes to form a dragon.

Carp Fish Cutout Pattern

Carp Fish
for Crepe Paper Fish Prints

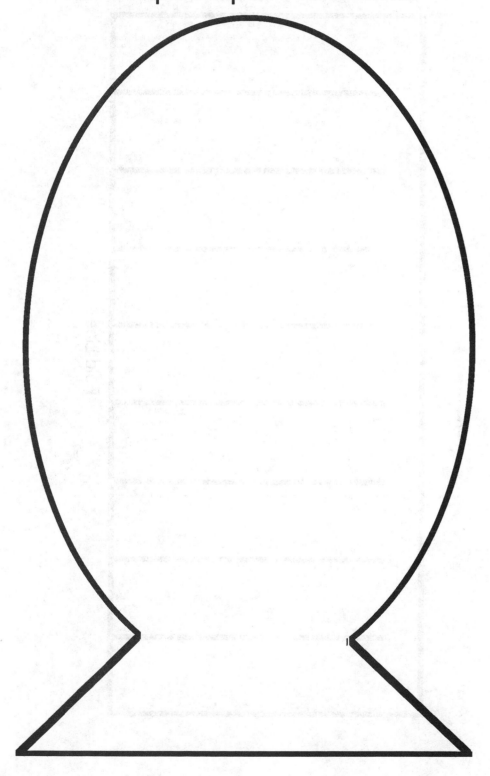

Lantern Pattern
Fold Paper in half. Cut on lines.

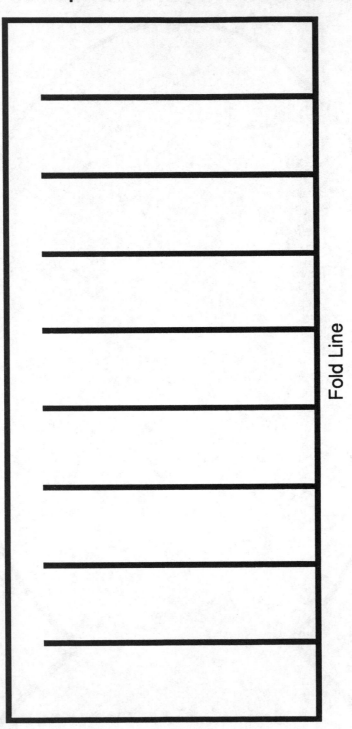

Fold Line

Vietnamese Hat Cutout Pattern

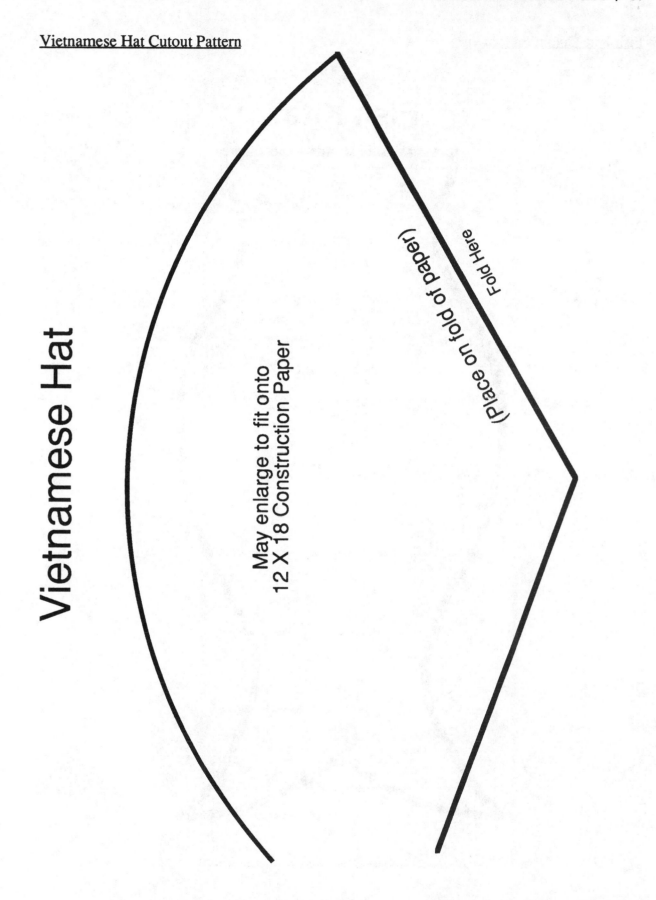

Vietnamese Hat

May enlarge to fit onto
12 X 18 Construction Paper

(Place on fold of paper)

Fold Here

Fish Kite Cutout Pattern

Fish Kite

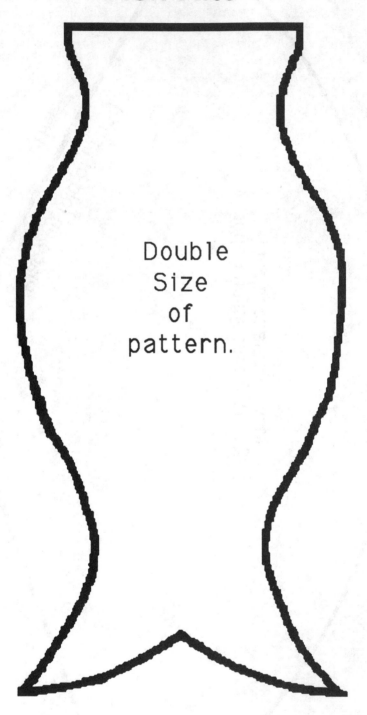

Double
Size
of
pattern.

Hawaiian Culture

by Cathy Higa

Hawaii is more than just a luau; more than a necklace of flowers. It has its own language, culture, art forms, and way of life. It is a group of islands to which people have come from far away, joining those who have always lived there. It is important to present Hawaii to the child in a way that is tangible and easy to relate to. To start the study, I have found it helpful to draw a mural that first describes the oceans and volcanos. During the next day we add the formation of the islands. Through following days we discuss and add how plants come to the island, and later, animals and people (in canoes, etc.). Each new concept adds to the mural. Soon we see homes, people at work (farming or fishing, etc.), modes of transportation (canoes), clothing, dance, and art styles. The children can re-tell the story of Hawaii everyday beginning at the volcano.

Practical experiences and activities such as printing tapa or stringing a lei will reinforce that concept of the story mural. The children can experience more with hula skirts, plastic leis, shells, or wooden sticks available for dramatic play.

"Hawaii" reaches into every area of the early childhood curriculum: language, music, art, gross/fine motor, science, nutrition, and dramatic play. The following is a sampling of a child's Hawaii experience.

Count one to ten:

1—Kahi (KAH-hee)

2—Lua (LOO-ah)

3—Kolu (KOH-loo)

4—Ha (Hah)

5—Lima (LEE-mah)

6—Ono (OH-noo)

7—Hiku (HEE-koo)

8—Walu (WAH-loo)

9—Iwa (EE-wah)

10—Umi (OO-mee)

Hello:	Aloha (ahLOWhah)
Thank you:	Mahalo (mahHAHlow)
Dance:	Hula
Fish:	I'a (EEah)
Hurry:	Wikiwiki

Malihini Poi
(Banana Bread Pudding)

2 cups stale bread crumbs (no crusts)
2 cups scalded milk
1 Tb. sugar
1/2 Tb. salt
1 cup mashed bananas
1/4 cup melted butter
2 eggs slightly beaten

Soak bread in scalded milk and let cool. Add all other ingredients and bake in greased pudding dish for one hour at 325 degrees.

When cool this is the consistency that may be eaten with the fingers like poi.

Haupia
(Hawaiian Coconut Pudding)

3 cups coconut cream*
3 cups water
1/3 cup cornstarch
1/2 cup sugar
1/4 tsp. salt
dash vanilla

Mix all ingredients. Bring to a boil, stirring constantly. Boil until thickened, about 10 minutes. Pour into flat pan. Chill or let cool. Cut into squares.

* You may buy frozen coconut milk from an oriental food store or use fresh.

Song

HAWAIIAN RAINBOWS
(Traditional Children's Song)

Hawaiian Rainbows,

White clouds roll by;

You show your colors,

Against the sky.

Hawaiian Rainbows,

It seems to me,

Reach from the mountains,

Down to the sea.

Hawaiiana Chart #1

Hawaiiana #1
by Cathy Higa

	The people of Hawaii enjoy music and dancing.	The people of Hawaii grow and eat many foods. Hawaiian people eat outdoors and cook in an "imu"—an earth pit. Hot stones cook the food.	The people of Hawaii wear special costumes when they dance.	The people of Hawaii made clothing from plants and feathers.	The people of old Hawaii lived in grass thatched houses.
Concept					
Art Experience	Create an "ipu" with an empty and clean bleach bottle. Paint brown. Tap bottle on floor and with palm of hand.		Create a hula skirt. Staple newspapers to a stiff paper band. Paint green. Cut into 1" strips. staple around waist.	Children create imitation "tapa." Wet brown package paper. Crumble into a ball. Soak in mud & brown paint. Let dry. Open. Children print lines etc. onto tapa with brown, black, red paints.	Make a "Hale." Cut milk carton. Paint brown. Glue on grassroof or palm sides.
Science Experience	Examine natural materials used in Hawaiian instruments: shells, gourds, feathers, stones, etc.	Children examine and taste pineapple, papaya, coconut, guava, taro. Cut off crown of pineapple and plant in soil.	Gather flowers to sew a lei or cut paper flowers and alternate with straws.		Design a Hawaiian village replica. Paint on ocean, taro fields, coconut groves, fish ponds and hales.
Music and Movement	Listen to Hawaiian music. Dance to "Pupu Hinu Hinu" use shells and arm motions.	Children can adapt "Way Up High in the Guava Tree." They can pretend to be a seed and grow into a papaya tree.	Dance a hula: Two steps to the left, two steps to the right.		Create a "Hula Center." Put mats on the ground. Provide plastic leis, hula skirts, ipus, shells and wood carved bowls. Put scenic pictures on the walls too.
Fine Muscle		Cut and slice fruits.	Sew a lei. Hula motions.		
Large Muscle	"Pupu Hinu Hinu" arm motions of "ocean," "listening," and "sleeping."			Paint, soak, and prepare the tapa cloth.	
Language	Expose children to Hawaiian words. pupu = shell kai = ocean water lohe = listen moe = sleep	Write a "Taste Test" story. Let children dictate words describing the different fruit tastes.	Exposure to Hawaiian words. pau = finished umi'i = circle hips around.	The royalty in Hawaii wore feather cloaks. Tapa was used mainly for clothing and house coverings, like blankets. Read *Kahala* by Guy Buffet or *Kamapua'a* by Guy and Pam Buffet.	Continue exposure to words. hale = house Kumu = teacher Kupuna = elder
Special Activities		Cook Haupia: coconut pudding (see recipe).	Make headbands. Glue cut paper flowers to band of paper. Staple around child's head.		*Hawaii is a Rainbow*, by Stephanie Feeney.

Hawaiiana Chart #2

Hawaiiana #2
by Janice Sheffield

Concept	Hawaii was formed by a volcano.	Birds and the ocean brought seeds to the island.	People came to the Island to live.	Fish is a food that comes from the ocean.	Hawaii does not get cold—it is a good place to grow food.
Art Experience	Glue cone shape on heavy paper—red tissue paper to go out top, paint volcano black.	Make cymbals out of coconut half shells. Plant seeds in the shells.	Glue grass and sticks to hut—put up on wall.	Watercolor fish—put up on wall	Make a paper Lei: string a 1" straw; a paper flower, straw, paper flower, etc.).
Science Experience	Volcano—Place 1/4 cup vinegar in small jar - place in mound of dirt, add 1 Tb.. baking soda—watch it erupt!	Open up a coconut and taste.	Create a hula skirt. Staple newspapers to a stiff paper band. Paint green. Cut into 1" strips. staple around waist.	Fish with magnets (fish have paperclips on them).	Cut up fresh pineapple, papaya, mango, bananas, coconuts—have a salad for lunch.
Music and Movement	"Hawaiian Rainbows"	Pretend to be a bird hatching from an egg... flying to find food.	"Hawaiian Rainbows"	Put on hula skirt and lei and practice moving to Hawaiian music.	Make Malihina (banana bread pudding).
Fine Muscle		Make a bird feeder—pine cone, stuff with peanut butter and roll in bird seed.	Cut out huts.	Cut out fish.	
Large Muscle			Gather grass and sticks for art project.		Make a real flower lei—needle goes inside center of flower and out stem; give a lei to someone at the feast.
Language	Draw a picture to show how Hawaii was formed by a volcano.	On same picture add: How the birds brought seeds, the water brought coconuts, and they started to grow.	Then add: people came & started living there, made huts, brought dogs, pigs, & moa fowl.	Then add: how people made clothes from tree bark & long grass, they cooked outdoors and fished.	
Special Activities	Hibiscus on the table (state flower). Count the petals on the flower (from 1 to 5).	Science table—driftwood, shells, cork & net.			Have a feast outside (luau).

Ireland

by Janice Sheffield, Susan Hopkins, and Janey Marquez

Apart from St. Patrick's Day, the only time we may hear about Ireland is when there has been another episode of conflict and violence in the news. Children might have questions about these incidents that teachers will need to respond to appropriately. Children need to be reassured that although there are violent confrontations, there are people working on conflict management. Teachers can mention how children sometimes need to manage their conflicts. We need to remember not to give children more information than they are asking for, but to actively listen to their concerns.

Planning and implementing activities about Ireland, helps to bring the children to the understanding that the Irish, and Irish-Americans, have a proud heritage and are working to help their children grow to become productive, peaceful citizens of our world.

We tend to think of Ireland in relationship to St Patrick's Day. While it is a holiday which is great fun to celebrate, we need to remember that Irish culture, like all cultures, is much more that just the celebration of holidays. Irish culture is also:
—folksongs and dances; lively and hauntingly beautiful;
—imaginative creatures such as leprechauns and faerie folk;
—people who are proud of their cultural traditions such as "kissing the Blarney Stone."

Ireland is an island. It is green and rolling, with high cliffs in the west and hills all over. When people from Ireland want to remember their island, they wear green because Ireland is very green with vegetation, due to the heavy rainfall and the cool climate all year long.

Irish people often wear a shamrock because it has become a national symbol of Ireland. The shamrock is considered by many people to bring good luck. Be sure to look at shamrocks in the daytime because they close their leaves in the evening.

People greet each other in Ireland with the traditional Irish greeting, "Top of the Morning." But…should you hear a wee small voice and turn around to find a tiny old man, beware! It could be a tricky and mischievous leprechaun. (Leprechauns are shoemakers for all the other faerie folk, you know.) If you are quick, you might catch one. Remember to look the leprechaun steadily in the eye for then he will be forced to reveal the location of his pot of gold. The leprechaun can escape if you relax your gaze.

We had a leprechaun visit our school one week last year. Each day when we came into class we discovered that he had pulled some trick on us. He left our room a mess, and he even turned our milk green! One day we found his wee little hat and jacket. We wrote the leprechaun a note telling him how we were feeling about his tricks and he finally learned how to be a helpful leprechaun.

The children were delighted by this naughty little imaginary creature who caused all sorts of mischief. Through this creation they were able to use their imaginations, express their feelings verbally, and have a great deal of fun!

We can bring Irish culture into our daily activities as we discuss the weather, as we prepare and eat potatoes, as we create with our imaginations, and learn folksongs. It is important to help the children repeatedly to make the connections of similarities in cultures as we move through the year.

Irish Soda Bread

2 cups flour
1 tsp. baking powder
1/2 tsp. baking soda
1/2 tsp. cream of tartar
1 Tb. caraway seeds
3/4 cup nonfat buttermilk

In a medium bowl stir together the dry ingredients.

Make a well in the center, pour the buttermilk into it and mix well.

Knead the dough about a dozen times in the bowl. If it is too dry to form into a ball, work in a little more buttermilk.

Spread the bottom of a pie pan with cornmeal.

Flatten the ball into a circle 7" in diameter and place it in the pan.

Cut an "X" about 1/4" deep, dividing the dough into fourths.

Bake in a preheated oven at 400 degrees until browned, about 50 minutes.

Makes 1 loaf.

Ireland Chart

Ireland
by Janice Sheffield

Concept	Potatoes are a main food in Ireland.	The Shamrock reminds people of Ireland.	Bread that people eat in Ireland.	Many Irish people eat fish.	In Ireland men use a shillelagh—a special walking stick.
Art Experience	Make a Blarney Stone from a medium size box. Do potato printing.	Make a Shamrock from 3 green hearts - look at pattern; add paper rocks to Ireland map.	Make cows to go on large Ireland "map."	2 pieces of waxed paper with shape of fish traced on, starch tissue paper between, cut out "fish" when dry.	Make a shillelagh from heavy paper (roll the paper, then twist).
Science Experience	Start growing a potato by putting half in water - hold in place with toothpicks.		Make Irish soda bread - eat at lunch time.	Fishing with magnets (the "fish" have paperclips on the nose).	
Music and Movement	Irish music	Practice kissing the Blarney Stone using the "crab walk" position. ↑	↑	↑	
Fine Muscle	Green playdough for free play.	Draw a leprechaun on paper with the Shamrock. ↑	Knead the dough. ↑	↑	
Large Muscle	Put paper on Blarney Stone (box) to make it look like a rock.	Practice the "crab walk."			
Language	Locate Ireland on the map - notice it is an island of very rocky ground.	Talk about Leprechaun real or pretend; Shamrock; "Top of the Morning" = hello.	Note from Leprechaun - lost his hat & jacket.	Children write a note to Leprechaun about mess he makes.	Go for a walk and use the shillelagh; notice all the vegetation around us.
Special Activities	Ireland is green with vegetation - lots of rain & cool all year around; display a wall map of Ireland.	Children discover room messed up - a tiny jacket was left behind, the milk at lunch turned green.	Children discover room messed up, again- a tiny hat was left behind, more green milk.		Shillelagh (shi-LAY-lee) crooked wooden stick they carry as a cane.

Jewish Culture. Thoughts on Jewishness

by Viki Diamond

Although is it extremely difficult to separate Jewish life and culture from religious belief and practice for the purposes of this book, I do believe that American Jewry has contributed much to the diverse culture of these United States.

Bearing firmly in mind the developmental needs of young children, two of the most important practices to which the Jewish community was (and is) committed were the central value of an intact and vigorous family life and the celebration of joy. In this, an abundance of food, the sharing of song and dance, and the absolute rules of hospitality to all, especially those less fortunate, are worth noting.

One of the fundamental concepts of peace education is that we work together to ensure the safety of our children and this was paramount in Jewish family life. The security of the family, the abiding sense of community, the affirmation of children themselves as the future and legacy of all, and the sense of joy with which occasions were marked continue today in Jewish homes.

Concepts: family life where everyone contributes and all are welcome.

Art: the development of language and use of clay.

Science: potatoes are as important to Jewish families as to Irish families particularly at Hanukkah time, when children eat potato pancakes with sour cream.

Music and Movement: Singing and dancing includes everyone from the oldest to the youngest and dances are most often in lines or circles so everyone can join in. Whenever anything needs celebrating, a hora is danced for it.

Fine muscle: make a four-sided dreidle (top). Play the game.

Large muscle: dancing.

Language: one of the nicest words Jews say all over the world is "Shalom." It means "Peace" and people say it when they meet and when they part. At dinner time, when all the family is gathered, they say "L'chaim!" It means "To Life."

Special activities: in the early days of America, many Jewish men were traders and peddlers and went all over the country selling everything you could imagine. There were often no roads, no maps, and no bridges in the wilderness. If you were a peddler, where would you go and what would you sell to people who could never-ever get to a store because there were none? How would you trade with people who had no money?

Faith and practice are as much combined in Hopi and other Native American cultures as they are in that of Jewish families. I do think there should be an attempt to show this in the experiences we provide young children. Teachers and caregivers in multiethnic situations would be wise to concern themselves with the many other ethnic groups in which religion and family life tradition and ritual are so closely interwoven as to be virtually inseparable.

Modern-Day Latkes

6 medium-sized potatoes
1 small onion
2 small zucchini—optional
1 medium-large carrot—optional
1 egg, beaten
3 Tbs. flour
1/2 tsp. baking powder

Grate potatoes in food processor, adding onion at the end. Add veggies if desired.

Remove to a bowl and press out potato juice.

Add the beaten egg, flour and baking powder.

In *heavy* (or electric) skillet, fry by rounded teaspoons, flattening down as indicated. Use peanut or safflower oil and have it HOT.

Drain on absorbant paper.

Serve with applesauce, sour cream, maybe a pickle...?!

Nicaraguan Culture

by Susan Hopkins

Nicaragua, you might think, would be a difficult culture to study with young children. However, it is one that they hear about on the news…and it's one that is relatively close by. We feel it's important not to be scared off by cultures which are struggling to survive. Children can and should hear a little about the war (not politics, rather how hard life can be in a war-torn country). Shielding children from reality won't prevent wars.

On a brighter side, Nicaragua has some wonderful cultural traditions for us to enjoy sharing with children. Craft, food, and music ideas follow and we hope you'll take this opportunity to help children learn about a culture not so commonly studied in this country.

The activities suggested for Nicaragua can serve as examples of types of activities that can be done for any Central or South American country. If you have any natives from South American countries in your classes, you might encourage them to participate by sharing information about their cultural heritage. Appropriate activities, books representing the area, and recipes of foods can be provided. The children's parents can often help provide these things. Teachers, however, should beware of stereotyping, such as assuming that these children speak Spanish.

Actively involving children in doing something to connect them to children in another country is another way to provide concrete experiences and model social responsibility. One of the positive ways we can help the people of Nicaragua is through the Madre program. Madre is based in New York and is a program which coordinates sister schools in the United States and in Nicaragua. We send our "twin" school a huge package a couple of times a year. Parents, children, and teachers work hard to earn money to buy much-needed supplies such as paper, crayons, diapers, and even mats for napping. The children do chores at home to earn money, they do drawings at school which are made into notecards for selling, and they hold bake sales. Their teachers help them select from catalogs which can be bought with the money they've earned. The teachers pre-select pictures that correspond to the amount which can be spent, and then the children choose. It's all a very real lesson in helping others and it's also a lesson in economics!

Nicaraguan Culture Chart

Nicaraguan Culture by Val Buckie

Concept	Nicaraguan children enjoy rice & beans as a main source of food.	Children in Nicaragua cook differently & eat without knives & forks.	Children everywhere enjoy the same kinds of fun, stories, art, letters!	Children all over the world enjoy planning parties!!	Children all over the world enjoy parties. Have a Fiesta!
Art Experience	Glue a bean & rice collage on a paper map of Nicaragua.	Work with clay: create bowls, plates, cups.	Glue tissue paper on the Piñata.	Weave colorful placemats for the fiesta. Finish piñata.	Decorate the class for a fiesta.
Science Experience	Grow beans by planting them on a paper towel in window.		Measure & mix flour & water to glue piñata.	Find place to hang piñata, talk about tying knots & try on the blindfold.	
Music and Movement		Sing class traditional songs in Spanish. Example: "Clean up Time"	Continue to sing songs in Spanish.	Sing and dance along with Spanish music. Play instruments.	Continue to sing class songs in Spanish.
Fine Muscle	Gluing beans; planting beans.	Grating cheese; molding clay.	Attaching tissue to piñata.	Weaving.	Tape the decorations up around room.
Large Muscle	Move body parts one at a time and make a room chart to label body parts in Spanish.			Swing at the large piñata for practice only.	Really try to break piñata open.
Language	Translate some simple words such as: table = mesa; books = libros; hand = mano. Use large sign around room.	Translate songs together.	Write a letter to a "twin" center in another country.		Write invitation poster in Spanish to other classrooms for "fiesta" today.
Special Activities		Cook cheese quesadillas.		Prepare punch & cookies for party.	Have a fiesta with the children & babies from other classes.

Spanish Songs

CALABASA

Halloween is "Calabasa" sung to the tune of "Frère Jacques"

Calabasa, calabasa
Muy chistosa, muy chistosa
Dos ojos grandes, dos ojos grandes
No le tengo miedo, no le tengo miedo

This repeats changing to

Una nariz grande, una nariz grande
Una boca grande, una boca grande

HELLO SONG

A Hello song in Spanish,   Tune: "Frère Jacques"   Repeat each line.

Good day, good day,
How are you?
Very well, thank you.
And yourself?

Buenos dias, buenos dias
¿Como estas? ¿Como estas?
Muy bien, gracias, muy bien gracias.
¿Y usted? ¿Y usted?

<u>Children and the World</u>

by Val Buckie

As an aspect of teaching global awareness it is important to enable young children to begin identifying with not only where they live, but to extend that into how they are involved in the larger world around them. For instance a child lives in Anaheim Hills, her school is in Fullerton, she lives in the state of California which is part of the United States, and the United States is one part of the world.

One way to help children begin to identify with people from other cultures is to start a "Sister School" program. The following steps will be helpful in starting such a program at your center. Penpals can be found through:

A. Madre (212) 627-0444;
B. Parents and people who have come from other countries;
C. Cultural groups in your community.

Penpal and sister school activities:

1. Show children, using a globe or map, where their penpals live in comparison to their own home.

2. Discuss the environment of that country. Show pictures of what the surrounding landscape and the people look like. Talk about similarities and differences of the people there and the people in their own lives.

3. Write a letter. Draw pictures with captions. Take photographs of your school with the children in the pictures. Let the children narrate what their school activities are like.

4. Have the letter translated if necessary.

5. Mail something to your penpals frequently—allow lots of time for them to write back. Try not to become discouraged if it takes some time for your sister school to make contact with you. Keep in mind that the mail systems in other parts of the world may not be as developed as ours. Explain this to the children if appropriate.

6. Make a tape recording of songs and children's comments if your sister school has a tape player.

7. Gather the children around once a week and discuss your sister school. Let the children verbalize what they know about other cultures and countries.

8. Share all correspondence with the children and post any photographs or artwork done by the "sister" children in the classrooms and lobby of your center. Translate if necessary.

Pedal for Peace! A Trike-a-thon

by Betsy Gibbs

Why? To have fun and raise money to help someone who needs help. To realize that we can work hard and share with people who need our help.

How? Four weeks in advance: Choose a location and select a coordinator and helpers, for jobs such as:

> Decorations
> Signs
> Buttons
> Trike decoration
> First aid
> Thirst aid (pit stop)
> Registration table
> Bake sale
> Counters and a starter
> Publicity
> Pledge sheet

Three weeks in advance: get all the signs ready for the areas, make numbers for the children's backs, and have children paint murals to hang on nearby fences, trees, etc. Contact the press. Line up photographers. Remind people to get their pledges.

One week in advance: Be sure all helpers understand their jobs. Remind all riders when to come, where to park, what to bring.

That morning: Set up an hour before it starts. Have a station for children to decorate their trikes. Have a separate section for two-wheelers. Set up bake sale and coffee for onlookers. Start the children in "waves." Have counters mark each child's back as they pass a check point. Tally the marks at the end, and record each child's success. Estimate the earnings. Stop everyone after half an hour for a group photo, rest, and then start up again if desired.

Afterwards: Each child (parent) collects the pledges and turns them in by your deadline. Post photographs. Announce your success, and let everyone know how you will benefit your selected group.

CSUF Children's Center raised over $900 in its first 1-1/2 hour Trike-A-Thon to benefit a "twin" daycare center in Managua, Nicaragua.

United Nations Chart

United Nations
by Susan Hopkins and Viki Diamond

Concept	Peace Day is a celebration of the meaning of peace.	Our world is home to all people.	Peace means solving problems in a way that is fair to everyone.	The United Nations helps countries solve their problems peacefully.	The U. N. helps children all over the world.
Art Experience	Make streamers to decorate the peace balloons.		Problem-solve distribution of art materials with children as they collage, paint, etc.	Make angry/happy pictures. Discuss feelings.	Make posters to announce UNICEF bake sale.
Science Experience		Introduce the globe—discuss geophysical areas such as mountains, deserts, islands and discuss how people have adapted their lives to living in those places.		Learn how the U.N. helps people with food and medical care.	
Music and Movement	Learn peace songs listed in Celebrations of Peace chapter (or other peace songs).	Listen to music from several different countries.	See tapes of Peace Songs by Red Grammer, Viki Diamond, and Sarah Pirtle.		Act out "One Light, One Sun" by Raffi.
Fine Muscle	Make and decorate cut out cookies in the shape of peace doves.	Make a paper maché model of our world.		Decorate the U. N. flag.	Make peace cookies for the bake sale.
Large Muscle		Practice moving as if you live in the mountains where you must climb, swimming, if you live near water.		Play non-competition games—see Cooperative Sports and Games.	
Language	Discuss meaning of "peace." Role play conflict management situations.	Learn to say "hello" in several different languages.	Problem solving books: I Want It; My Name Is Not Dummy by Elizabeth Crary.	Continue to role play conflict management.	Raffi Songs to Read, "One Light, One Sun."
Special Activities	Have a celebration, sing peace songs, have a picnic, light Peace Candle.	Read A New True Book: United Nations by Carol Green (see bibliography).		Invite a visitor from your local U. N. chapter.	Send bake sale proceeds to UNICEF. Include letter explaining how money was raised and why.

APPRECIATION OF THE ENVIRONMENT

by Laurie Winters

Children can begin to learn at a young age to appreciate the environment in which they live. Respect for the preservation of the earth and the vast systems which reside upon it is a value that must be taught if humanity is to continue to live as a healthy species.

We can teach children about conservation, ecology, the places where the foods we eat come from, and much more. Young children can begin to learn the concept of conservation through everyday activities such as picking up after themselves, throwing away trash, reusing materials rather than throwing them away, and taking good care of materials and possessions. Children need to be encouraged to take care of things and time should be allowed for such activities.

The acquisition of this knowledge will enable them to think of the earth as a place that is to be cherished and lived with, rather than a place to be dominated. Following are activities to support learning to appreciate our home, the earth.

Appreciation of Environment Chart

Appreciation of Environment — by Laurie Winters

Concept	Growing things enrich the environment.	All living things have important jobs to help our earth.	Our earth is very special.	The earth belongs to all of us—all living creatures.	Earth is our home—we need to take care of it.
Art Experience	Explore various foods such as melons, peppers. etc. by taste, smell, feel.	Make a paper ladybug—cutting, gluing spots & legs.	Make clay pottery or artifacts.		Make two murals—one to fill with trash, one for natural "treasures".
Science Experience	Plant radish seeds or grass in cups.	Talk about & show live ladybugs - their role in our ecological structure, "how they help."	Display various types of soil - clay, sand, etc. Feel and discuss; may add water to change consistency.	Nature walk to observe trees, bugs, birds, etc. & discuss their roles.	Fill sand table with water—children bring items in each day to add "pollution" to water.
Music and Movement	Movement Game: "All the Little Seeds" by Clare Cherry.	Pretend to be ladybugs.	Navajo music & dances. Carlos Nakai—flute.	Tape: *The Wind is Telling Secrets*—by Sarah Pirtle.	
Fine Muscle		Hold ladybugs very gently.	Sand paintings. Show examples of Native American ones.	Nature collage—gather leaves, etc. from the ground.	
Large Muscle	"Grow Little Seed" Pretend to be seeds and then grow up into various plants.	Make a garden to take care of.			Go on an "exploring walk" and pick up trash and natural treasure—put in bags.
Language	Learn the names of several new foods.	Discuss various roles of plants & animals & why they are needed.	*When Clay Sings* by Byrd Baylor.	*Once There Was a Tree* by Ramonova.	Discuss which materials are biodegradable—why?
Special Activities			Bring in a Native American visitor.	Collect insects with children, being sure not to keep them long.	

<u>How Plants Grow Chart</u>

How Plants Grow   by Melissa Steubing

Concept	All green plants need water, soil and sunlight.		Plants grow in different ways: some from seeds; some from cuttings.	Plants have parts such as seeds, roots, leaves.	
Art Experience	Cut out and glue collage pictures: what seeds turn into i.e. carrot, corn, flowers.	Make collage with different kinds of seeds.	Trace sequential bean development pictures.	Cut out sequential bean development pictures.	Children will make bulletin boards from bean pictures.
Science Experience	Sensory tubs: soil, water, various seed types.	Plant grass seeds in egg shells.	Plant potato eyes in juice can—3 holes in bottom for drainage.	Plant beans in cut off milk carton.	
Music and Movement	Learn new song "A Little Seed for Me to Sow...."				Pretend to be a seed, pretend to plant and take care of seed. Grow like a plant.
Fine Muscle	Plant seeds: take care of them by watering, etc.				
Large Muscle			Hammer nails to build outside planter box.	Fill outside planter box with dirt - wheelbarrow and shovels.	Till the soil, plant seeds, then water soil.
Language	Read *How a Seed Grows* by Jordan.	Have several seed growing books available to look at.	Read *Bean Seeds and More Seeds* by Selsam.	Read *The Hidden Magic of Seeds* by Shuttlesworth.	Read *The Plant Sitter* by Zion.
Special Activities	Involve parents in acquiring seeds, soil, wood, advice, etc. for planter box.	Experiment with growing sprouts, eat them for a snack.	Grow a sweet potato in glass of water supported by toothpicks.	Grow avocado in glass jar—children can observe root formation.	Take field trip to a local nursery, strawberry patch, or pumpkin patch.

Water Conservation Chart

Water Conservation   by Janice Sheffield

Concept	We need to use our water wisely.	We use water in many different ways.	Every living thing must have water to live.	Plants need water to grow.	Water - great home for many wildlife.
Art Experience	Water color.	Chalk and water.			
Science Experience	Let the faucet drip into a container, then check in 15 minutes to see how much was captured.	Make stone soup (have children bring in different things for the soup).	Classroom terrarium - fix the soil and get it ready for planting.	Finish terrarium, plant ferns, seeds, or plants. Make individual terrarium out of sandwich bags. Add wet potting soil, plant 3-4 beans, close bag.	Look at pond water through a pond scope (put pond water in large container).
Music and Movement	Act out something we do with water, others guess what the person is acting out.	Tape: *The Wind is Telling Secrets*—song "Sitting in the Soup."	Pretend to be a worm.		Pick up litter around the pond (not too close to the pond).
Fine Muscle	Practice how to wash hands and then turn the water off at group time.		After walk - let children pour themselves a glass of water.	Mix the potting soil and water in small container.	Look at the pond water level, what can a fish see?
Large Muscle		Act out ways we use water.	Go for a walk and gather small pebbles. Look for small plants, moss for terrarium.		Visit a pond.
Language	How much water do we waste when we don't turn the water off after washing our hands?	Read *Stone Soup*. (many versions available)	What do plants need to grow?	What happens if you overwater a plant? (overwater teacher's plant)	What can you see in the water? What is growing around the pond? Look for tracks around the pond.
Special Activities		Make a solar still in sandbox area (see instructions following).		Is this a wise way to use water (overwatering) ?	

Terrarium

by Janice Sheffield

(Here's a garden that makes its own rain)

To make a terrarium, find a big jar or an old fishbowl. Make sure your hand can fit into the opening. A jar turned on its side gives more planting space. To keep a round jar from rolling, make a base from a big, thick plastic sponge. Wet the sponge to soften it, then lay the jar in place on it. Let the sponge dry completely. The weight of the jar presses the sponge into the right shape for the base.

Prepare for planting by spooning in a one-inch layer of pebbles and sand. Use potting mix or, for a desert scene, soil mixed half and half with sand. Add a couple of interesting rocks for decoration, pressing them firmly into the soil.

If the soil is dry, moisten it, but not too much. Mist with a hand sprayer. Close the jar and let it stand overnight for the moisture to spread through the soil. If your jar has no lid, cover the opening with transparent plastic held in place with string or a rubber band.

What to Plant:

Ferns, tiny tree seedlings or other small outdoor plants;

Buy some small potted plants;

Plant the tops of carrots, beets, turnips. Plant some seeds.

Decide where each plant will go, then spoon out a small hole in the soil, just big enough for the plant and its dirt clump. Set the plant in place and gently press down dirt around it with back of a spoon. Push seeds in with the point of a pencil.

Give a quick mist with the sprayer to settle the soil. If you need to clean the sides of the terrarium, wipe down gently with tissue. Add a garden insect or two if you like.

Place the terrarium where it gets plenty of light, but not direct sun. It should seldom need watering; it makes its own rain. Moisture condenses on the glass, then is reabsorbed by the soil. If it appears dry, spray in a little mist. If it seems to be drippy, or mildew starts, remove the cover and let it dry out a bit.

Solar Still

Materials needed:

Plastic sheet (preferably clear), about 6' square

Container to collect the water

Collecting container

Small rock

In a sunny place, dig a cone-shaped hole about 20" deep and about 3' across. Place your collecting container in a depression in the center of the hole. Stretch plastic sheet over the hole and lightly weigh down the edges with dirt. Carefully place a small rock the size of your fist in the middle of the sheet so that it hangs down about 5" above the container. Make sure the plastic does not touch the insides of the hole at any place. Add more dirt on the edges of the plastic to hold it in place. In a couple of hours, water should begin to collect.

The solar still works on sun power. The heat of the sun evaporates moisture from the soil, which then condenses on the plastic sheet. As it condenses, it runs down to the lowest point under the rock, then drips into the container. If you are on a beach near the ocean, fresh water can be distilled from the sand.

National Wildlife Federation
1412 16th St. N.W.
Washington, D.C. 20036

California Natural Resources Federation
2775 Cottage Way, Suite 39
Sacramento, California 95825

Ideas to Help Fight Pollution

by Susan Knox

With more people will come more pollution, unless we work very hard and convince all people to do the same. Following are a few suggestions which can be used by families:

1. Don't buy or use styrofoam cups. Styrofoam is not biodegradable. Each piece takes 100 years to break down in the soil. When styrofoam is burned, gas is formed which causes holes in the ozone layer around the earth.

2. Have "garbage patrols." Tell the children how proud you are of their cleanup efforts and make a garbage collage.

3. Save egg cartons and other items to recycle for art and science projects. Parents can help teachers this way.

4. Recycle cans, bottles, newspapers, computer paper, etc.

5. Don't buy products that are not in biodegradable containers unless they can be recycled, e.g., glass, plastic, aluminum.

6. Ask the checker at the grocery store to pack your groceries in paper (not plastic) bags.

Children can learn about pollution with our good example and some discussion. We need to take care of our planet if it's going to be habitable in future generations.

Pollution Chart

Pollution

There are different kinds of pollution.   by Connie Denholm

		Water Pollution	Litter	Noise Pollution	Air Pollution
Concept	Pollution happens when people do not keep our natural world clean.				
Art Experience	Compare: • Litter Collage • Nature Collage		Decorate lunch bags for use as car trash bags.		Blow art.
Science Experience	Take a nature walk. Take a litter walk.	Fill a tank with clean water. Have children choose non-natural items to add to it; discuss the changes. Pour water collected from different areas (include pollution tank) through coffee filter; discuss results.	Sort litter collected on walk (plastic, paper, metal…).	• Tape record children during active/quiet play. Play back and discuss. • Record familiar sounds then play name that sound.	Spread Vaseline on paper and place in different areas of your school (kitchen, yard, etc.). Look at daily and discuss findings.
Music and Movement	"Give a Hoot" Pollution Song.			•Sing songs in loud and quiet voices. • Play charades.	Pretend to be a bird flying in clean/polluted air.
Fine Muscle					
Large Muscle			• Take a litter walk. • Play trash can basket ball.	Move around without making any noise/making lots of noise—tape record and discuss.	
Language	Wilson's World by Edith Hurd.	The Lorax by Dr. Suess. Discuss how the characters feel.	Post children's comments about litter clean-up for parents and others to see.	Too Much Noise. Read it, then act it out.	
Special Activities		Start an aquarium in your room.		Have a whisper snack!	

Poem: <u>"In The Oval Garden."</u>

IN THE OVAL GARDEN
by Susan Knox

In the oval garden,

I'm bustin' sod, pioneering fantasy.

It's blistering hot so I turn the soil
    in a line down the middle.

I'll just do half today;

Then I bite off another piece.

I'll just do a sixth,

and I pry up the dry turf
    and stand back to rest.
    How much can my back stand of this?

Will I ever get seeds planted?

Gathering my breath, I see

part of a peace sign.
    That takes me back twenty years
    to when I was afraid to go on marches.

Just for fun, I finish the sign.

The gardens of the forties

were victory gardens
    and Gramma weeded in a long skirt, hat, and gloves.

Finished, unfinished
    I've done something special
    and I lean on the shovel handle
    admiring my work.

Five-year-old, raggle-taggle, genuine Jordon
    comes by and stops, confused.
    "What are you doing (you crazy old lady)?"

"I'm making a peace sign for the airplanes to see."

"What's peace?" inquires Jordon, squinting.

CURRENT EVENTS

On March 24, 1989 there was a disastrous oil spill near Valdez, Alaska. Nearly 11 million gallons of oil was spilled into Prince William Sound and contaminated 300 miles of shoreline. While this is certainly a grown-up problem, young children can learn about it and can help in some small ways with the clean-up. Following are some ideas for discussion and action which can be used as starting points in similar types of disasters. Such activities help children realize that they can contribute, take action, and be empowered.

The Alaskan Oil Spill

By Connie Denholm

What happened?
Clip articles from magazines and newspapers to share and discuss with children.
Make a simple flannel board story to depict the problems.
Locate Alaska on the map.

What is oil? What is it used for?
Visit a gas station.
Make a collage of things that use or are made from oil.

The effects:
Talk about the creatures in the area (what's happened to them and their home).
Discuss damage to plants and beaches.
Look at pictures from magazines and tape news clips on the subject.
Mix oil with water and note results.
Relate oil/water experiment to fish in classroom aquarium (oil sticks to the fish).

Look at beach tar.
Heat it up and notice how sticky it is; notice the smell.

What now? What can we do?
Talk about how oil is being cleaned from water, from beaches, and from animals.

Have children dip their fingers in oil, then have them wash their hands.
Notice how much work it is to get hands clean.

Ask children if they would like to earn some money to send to Alaska to help hire more people to help clean up the mess (it's important to ask, not tell, the children).
Offer ideas for their approval (it's their project, not yours).
Bake cookies, brownies, etc. for a bake sale. Do art work to be made into cards; marble painting; crayon ironing. Make a sign and have the children decorate it.
Have the children sell the items! It's important that the children know why they are selling and can tell prospective buyers.
Count the money from the sale with the children.

Follow up:
Send earnings with a letter dictated by the children to the clean-up fund. Hopefully you will receive a reply which is most satisfying to all your hard workers!
Post total earnings so that parents are aware of the outcome.

Cleaning Up Our World Chart

Cleaning Up Our World
by Connie Denholm and Susan Hopkins

Concept	We can help clean up litter.	We can help others to help clean up litter.	We can help with other cleanup projects.	We can recycle materials: aluminum, plastic, newspaper, glass.	We can make our living spaces beautiful.
Art Experience	Make "Litter Bags" for families to use. Decorate.	Make posters asking others not to litter.	Make a poster to depict cleanup needs.	Decorate boxes for recycling areas.	Decorate spaces, indoor and outdoor, with pretty materials.
Science Experience	Collect natural and synthetic materials—discuss and compare.	Make recycled paper from used paper towels, etc.	Learn about a place such as Alaska, which needs help with cleanup.	Classify and sort materials for recycling.	Plant and take care of a garden.
Music and Movement		Sing "We've Got the Whole World in Our Hands" as the globe is passed from child to child.			Use music to listen to and dance to for enjoyment.
Fine Muscle	Make two collages—one of natural & one of man-made materials.		For bake sale, make muffins, etc.	Melt crayons to make new ones.	Create handmade decorations.
Large Muscle				Visit a recycling center to take materials for recycling.	Children clean up own materials.
Language	Identify materials and label what they are made from.	Vocabulary such as litter, recycle, etc.	Vocabulary relating to a current environmental need.	*About Garbage and Stuff* by Ann Z. Shanks.	Read *Miss Rumphius* by Barbara Cooney.
Special Activities			Have a bake sale to earn money to send to a special project.	Use money earned from recycling for a special clean up project.	Celebrate the beauty of our world.

CONCERNS OF PEACE

<u>Peace Education For Young Children</u>

or, <u>Making Grown-up Concerns Developmentally Appropriate For Young Children</u>

by Susan Hopkins

Sometimes people express concern that "peace education" is not an appropriate topic for young children. My feeling is that it all depends upon how one defines "peace education". If one is planning a discussion of nuclear war, I would agree; young children are not yet developmentally ready for a topic which is both extremely ambiguous and scary. Peace education for young children also does not involve activities such as protest marches on military bases. These are grown-up activities and not appropriate for children who need concepts which build upon their own real-life experiences, and activities which expand those concepts.

What, then, is peace education for young children? Peace education develops first from self awareness and ultimately to global awareness by means of a carefully planned, experiential curriculum. As always, with young children we help them develop understanding through their own experience. We work with the following basic structure as a foundation:

• Self Awareness
  • Who am I?
  • How am I unique?
  • How am I like other people?
  • How can I best express my feelings?
  • How can I get my needs met?
  • How am I lovable?
  • How am I capable?

• Awareness of Others:
  • How can I make friends?
  • How can I be a friend?
  • How can we help others?
  • How are we alike and different?

• Getting Along with Others:
  • How can we express our needs and feelings?
  • How can we talk about problems?
  • What new ideas can we create for solving problems?

• Awareness of Global Society:
  • How are we the same and different from people who live in other countries?
  • How are we the same and different from people who are older, younger, a different color, a different gender, or who may have a disability?
  • How can we create new ways of enjoying our interactions with our global community?

• Environmental Awareness:
  • How can we take care of our land, air, and water?
  • How can we use our imaginations to create solutions to problems like pollution?

After the foundation is laid, we can work on some of the more challenging and often emotional issues such as conflict management, prejudice, and pollution. Adults must create an environment which is supportive and non-judgmental. It needs to be planned to help children develop understanding through concrete experiences to which they can relate from their daily lives. The adult must know the children well: have listened to their concerns, have watched how they play out their concerns, and have been alert to what activities the children may now be ready to tackle to help them grow.

Conflict management is a grown-up idea which can be worked on successfully with young children. We talk about "solving problems" with them rather than "negotiation" or "conflict resolution." With adult support, children can practice the steps of problem-solving.

1. Express everyone's feelings verbally.

2. Find out what happened.

3. Define the problem.

4. Think of solutions and consequences.

5. Plan and implement a solution.

6. Evaluate and adjust as needed.

Problem-solving is a very real and important part of how we live our lives. It is critical that children learn very early that problem-solving can be interesting, challenging, successful, and help to build relationships. It's a real opportunity to be creative. Children become empowered as they learn to solve problems.

We don't discuss "prejudice" and "stereotyping" with the children; rather we talk about and work on "fairness". We ask questions and relate discussions of issues as to whether or not that was a fair way to treat another person, and how the person felt about the treatment. An example of this concept being developed can be found in the following activity description. Using paper dolls of various colors, have all the purple dolls sit in the back of the room far away from where a story is being read to the other dolls. The purple dolls do not want to sit there, since they can not see the pictures, but that is the rule—all dolls who are purple must sit in the back. How do those dolls feel? How would you feel if you had to sit there? Is this a fair way to treat some dolls? The children are asked to consider the feelings and needs of other people, as well as themselves, through these activities.

Another example relating to fairness comes to mind as I recall how the four-year-old children had trouble accepting one in their group. The child had been badly burned in a fire. Before the children understood the situation they rejected the one who had been burned because they feared "catching her skin disease", feared hurting her by holding her hand, and generally did not want to be near her. Once she told the children about what had happened (with the teacher's support) and how the doctors are helping, they came to relate to her as another friend. They now understand.

Another grown-up concept which the children really relate to well and enjoy is that of "pollution." The concepts are made concrete with examples of litter, water pollution, and other forms of environmental contamination. Children can work hard to make our world a healthier, safer, and more beautiful place by learning to clean up after themselves, by learning not to waste resources, and by developing an appreciation of the natural environment.

Peace education must begin when children are very young. The grown-ups in their lives can work with these concepts to make them understandable by relating them to the experiences of the children and by developing them in active and concrete ways. Children can learn how to successfully work with some of our society's biggest problems. We can empower them to make a difference in our world. And we must empower them since this is their world too.

Gun Play

by Susan Hopkins

The issue of "gun play" is one to which parents and teachers of young children must give serious thought. Traditionally, gun play has been banned at most pre-schools, the idea being that peaceful people do not solve problems with guns. However, that concept is basically from the adult point of view, and recent research (Carlsson-Paige and Levin in *The War Play Dilemma*) indicates that children have important emotional needs which can be worked on through gun play; needs such as understanding fear, power, leadership, as well as good and evil, friends and enemies, and so on. Children may choose gun play because violence surrounds them on T.V. and in friends' play, and they want to try it out for themselves.

Unfortunately, banning tends to send behavior underground since banning means that the adult in charge simply won't get to see what's happening. When the children work on these issues openly, as they do in gun play, then we can observe their concerns and support them by discussion, problem-solving, and a variety of resources.

If you are feeling courageous, and willing to experiment with facilitating gun play rather than banning it, then you might care to consider the following ideas which are the result of similar courageous experimenting:

1. Read Carlsson-Paige and Levin's books, *Who's Calling the Shots* or *The War Play Dilemma*, for background and ideas to support children in these concerns and issues.

2. Meet with other adults who are involved with the children and have discussions about feelings and concerns.

Discuss questions such as:

   a. What are some of your earliest memories regarding gun/weapon play?

   b. Did you use play guns as a child?

   c. How was gun play handled when you were a child?

   e. What worries you about gun play?

In conclusion, make a list of the concerns expressed.

3. Give parents and staff some ideas for interventions such as are discussed by Carlsson-Paige and Levin. Situations will arise which are difficult to handle appropriately, and adults will need support in helping children deal with their issues, and also in protecting the rights of others in the group. Facilitating gun play does not give permission for a "free-for-all;" it means working through issues in ways which support the needs of everyone.

4. If you have had a policy of banning gun play, it would be helpful and much less confusing to the children if you would have a discussion with them about the changes which will be occurring. Such a discussion would be an excellent opportunity to mutually express feelings and concerns as well as some limit-setting in relationship to noise, how and where toy guns are used, etc. However, beware of putting so many limits on the play that you are, in effect, banning it.

5. Do some record keeping by using the "Gun Play Observation" form that appears later in this chapter (or a similar one) to get a handle on the issues on which the children are working. This information is valuable in planning appropriate learning opportunities to follow up on the children's issues and concerns.

6. If you are in a school setting, you may want to get some feedback from the parents by using the "Gun/Superhero Play Questionnaire" that appears later in this chapter. Parents are concerned about this issue and may well want to have a meeting to gain support and work on school policy.

The "gun play dilemma" is one of the serious questions we face in working with young children. However, it has potential for some exciting processes:

1. We can work with other adults to share feelings and problem-solve about policy;

2. Teachers and parents can support each other and learn new skills in working with children;

3. And best of all, we can do some real work with children as we relate to their concerns about their roles in the world. In all situations we can problem-solve, negotiate, share feelings, discuss, cooperate—all techniques of peace!

GUN/SUPERHERO PLAY QUESTIONNAIRE

Name_____ (optional)

1. Does your child engage in gun/superhero play at home? ____yes ____no

2. If no:

    a. Do you feel this is due to lack of interest on your child's part, or some other reason?

    b. What would you do if your child attempted to engage in this play?

3. If yes:

    a. How do you feel about this play?

    b. How do you respond to your child's play?

4. If your child watches TV cartoons, which are his/her favorites?

5. Do you see themes and characters from TV in your child's play? If yes, please describe.

6. Is there anything else you would like to tell us about this topic?

Please return to _____ basket by _____. !

THANK YOU SO MUCH!
(Adapted from Carlsson-Paige and Levin, *The War Play Dilemma*.)

GUN PLAY OBSERVATION FORM

By_____Date_____Time_____

Location_____Length of play if known_____

Children involved:G1_____G2_____G3_____G4_____

   B1_____B2_____B3_____B4_____B5_____

_____ DRAMATIC CONTENT OF PLAY:

_____Good guy/Bad-guy _____Cowboy ____Robbers _____Space _____Police

_____Other_____

      What evidence did you observe of the following (give child's code and behavior or verbal expression):

Power

Submission

Feelings of unfairness

Anger

Frustration

Inclusion

Exclusion

Leadership

Cooperation

Describe the weapons or imaginary weapons: What caused the play to stop or change?

Describe any interventions by adults and the effects.

Please write more if you have further descriptions or comments.

Constructive Ways to Facilitate War Play

Adults can help children expand and elaborate their play, including war play, using the following sample questions/responses. Always remember to listen and observe carefully to determine the issues with which the children are concerned. Your interventions must support and help the children work through their issues.

1. Support imaginative play by suggesting new ways to use props and play materials.

   "Maybe He-Man could use these Legos. That way he could trap the mud creature."

   "If you wore this cape, you could pretend to be a wizard. How do you think a wizard might help solve the problem?"

   "Does Cobra have a family? What does his family do when he is fighting? Let's draw pictures of Cobra's family. Let's build a home for Cobra's family in the block area."

2. Help with problem-solving by suggesting new roles or actions. Help children recognize consequences of their actions and those of others.

   "Poor Rambo. He only has one way of solving all of his problems. Let's help him. What else could he do?"

   "Rambo always seems to get what he wants by fighting. What are other ways he could get what he wants?"

3. Maintain the child's right to be original and creative.

   "You know, friends, Billy has never seen G.I. Joe. I think it would be interesting to let him bring in his unicorn if he wants to. How could his unicorn's magical powers protect G.I. Joe from Cobra?"

   "Does your monster have a special power that can help protect the 'good' guys from Cobra?"

4. Help children work through their issues by stepping in to guide the play. This can be an opportunity to help children realize that enemies are also people, to work with stereotypes, and to develop awareness of real versus pretend. But, beware of intruding and placing adult value judgements on children's themes.

   "Let's build a home for Cobra's family with these blocks."

   "Do bad guys have birthdays?"

   "Oh, Cobra is hurt. Can we find him a doctor?"

5. Ask open-ended questions to encourage thinking skills.

   "What would happen to the bad guys if our gun shot glue instead of bullets?"

   "Where does that bad guy go when he's not fighting with you?"

   "Can you tell me about how you made that weapon?"

   "How can you get Cobra to listen to you?"

6. Help children develop self-control by setting limits that keep play safe and manageable. Use opportunities to clarify real and pretend.

   "It's not okay to shoot Maria when she doesn't want you to. You may shoot at the pretend monster by the tree or you may find someone who wants to play that way."

   "Remember, Matt, Kyle is only pretending to be the bad guy; he isn't really bad."

   "I'm glad to see you and Michael are just pretending to hit, because if you really hit each other you'll both get hurt."

7. Help children practice conflict management skills. Role play and discuss:

> "The 'bad guys' got very angry today when the 'good guys' tried to capture their space ship. How did the 'bad guys' ('good guys') feel about it? What could the 'bad guys' have done besides pushing? What are some ways the 'good guys' could make a space ship of their own?"

8. Work with the children's issues, such as power, leadership, and friends, through a variety of activities.

> "Wow, that stuff looks really powerful! What's going into the potion? What else do you need to make it?" (Combine ingredients.)

> "Power is important. How do people get power? What is power?" (Discuss.)

> "Chris is our leader today. Leaders help us by setting out the napkins and cups, taking messages to the office, etc. What other jobs can leaders do?"

9. Use of children's literature in storytelling, puppets, dramatization, and discussion are also effective in helping children sort out their concerns, fears, and questions—and in helping them learn to cope. Some examples include:

> Sendak, *Where the Wild Things Are*
> de Paola, *The Knight and the Dragon*

Suggestions are taken from *The War Play Dilemma: Balancing Needs and Values in the Early Childhood Classroom* by Nancy Carlsson-Paige and Diane E. Levin.

People-Centered Discipline

by Viki Ann Diamond

I am coming to the conclusion that our children must be deeply rooted in nurturing humanism *very* early in their social lives. I call it "species awareness" and make it a top priority in my work. As folksinger, I work with groups of children in informally flexible assemblies. Care for one another in this setting is seen to be as important as the music, and the self-discipline of awareness is part of my own exercise of control.

It goes like this: During an assembly with singing and storytelling I often see one child who is "not with us." This poses no problem to me unless the child is disturbing others. If that is happening, I stop quietly and the following will likely ensue.

"My friend—with the red shirt. You are disturbing the kids around you, and I am not a TV set. When I sing I want to be listened to. Now, you have three choices. You may behave as you know you should and can, you may sit next to a teacher who will help you behave well, or we can make arrangements for you to leave. Which do you choose?"

Child decides to stay; they all do, and he sees very clearly that:
a) everyone is looking and listening and I am definitely not angry;
b) I expect an answer;
c) I have sent a clear message that non-punitive help is what I would expect from any intervening teacher.

Having gotten an "I'll behave" from the child, I say ". . . And you do know correct audience behavior, right?" Child nods. Then I turn to eyeball all the children in the immediate vicinity and say, "Now, you are all responsible for helping your friend not to get into trouble with his behavior." They look stunned and nod and right away (all this takes a very, very small bit of time) I go on with whatever I was singing or telling.

It is the last bit which teachers *and* children are getting back to me on. The behavior of one is the responsibility of all, in a non-punitive way. One child actually said in wonder, "Oh, *that's* how it works." And of course, I am not angry when presenting a child with his choices. I just point out that I am a human being who is here to be listened to.

These are most often pre-kindergarten, kindergarten, and first graders, occasionally older. What is just not being emphasized, it seems to me, is the whole-group positive—as opposed to negative—group responsibility for appropriate behavior. Too often it is the other way around. "Let's do this together so they won't find out (something)."

This may have ramifications for your explorations in other cultures. While it is good and also interesting to explore the differences between cultures and peoples, we may need to emphasize common humanities, common needs, common denominators at the early childhood level. We need to stress samenesses. One thing which has been happening consistently gives me hope and a lot to smile about. I use the song "Down On The Farm" a lot and children are asked to think quietly of two things which are so important to them they never want to be without. There is always a Quaker moment of silence to think in. Most times with the young children, parents, pets, and siblings come first; with teachers, food, and toys coming up next. Some children say "money" and there is always a wave of unease. Then I lead a brief discussion which curves around to the fact that work gets you money which can be used to help others. I never deny the child's choice, always affirm it, just broaden its scope. And again, teachers and children have gotten back to me with their thoughts on this.

Affirmation is a powerful tool, and children should be taught its message and use as soon as possible. Most school-based discipline is negative, and children need the strongest possible armor against the barrage. Nursery school is the place to start.

Countdown on Children's Television

by Pam Steinle

In the spring of 1987, I spent eight days viewing children's commercial television for a university course I teach on American culture and television. I applied little scholarly methodology—the rigor required was more along the lines of simple endurance as I watched as much television as I could whenever I could. I also taped several pre-selected programs which I needed to use in class along with course readings: *Popeye*, for example, as one of the earliest and longest running cartoon shows, and *Gobots* as one of the most successful new ones; *My Little Pony* and *Masters of the Universe*, as examples of toy-based/linked programs, and argued to be experienced as one unbroken advertisement, etc. In fact, my viewing and taping included commercials, since they are perceived in the same state of willing credibility that television programs induce and require in order to succeed.

Sadly, I expected, and was easily able to find extensive violent expression (in both number and range of violent actions), a low sense of consequence, even for the "bad guys," and rigid gender stereotyping. Commercials in particular emphasized and then offered consumer solutions to a world of social alienation—the perennial "make friends with Kool-Aid," buttressed by ads for "My Buddy," "Little Sister", and a multitude of talk-to and talk-back toys openly offered comfort and company for lonely, isolated preschoolers.

The composite picture and the sense of self depend in large part upon one's economic ability to purchase them. However, these aspects of children's television are not the focus of this essay. Each one is familiar as the topic of numerous publicized studies and arguments, *and* familiar as a high-tech version of our own television childhoods.

By contrast, what was shocking to me in viewing children's commercial television was the sustained portrayal of a universe in which nuclear warfare is a given. The premise of countless programs and commercials is that either a nuclear war is imminent and the heroes must strive, episode after episode, to head it off, —or—that a nuclear war has occurred and heroes live on an altered earth or have relocated elsewhere in the universe.

Examples of the first condition range from *Masters of the Universe*, *Gobots*, and *Defenders of the Earth* to *Rocky and Bullwinkle*, and even occasional episodes of *The Smurfs Adventures*. In several tapings that season, Tonka Toys advertised an armored vehicle—an apparent cross between a military tank and an ATV—the name of which I've forgotten, but the voice-over and landscape I haven't. In an obviously bombed-out desert and crater terrain, the "lyrical" refrain is "in the world outside, you drive to survive," and (face of young boy, sweat-smeared and alone, crawling up over a dune) "to stay alive, you drive to survive."

The second condition is not only exemplified in many of the futuristic/high-tech animated programs but also in those long-running favorites, *The Flintstones* and *The Jetsons*. Reflect for a moment and recognize that what is comforting, as much as comical, about both series is the perpetuation of suburban family life a la *Father Knows Best*—whether the family is "bombed back into the Stone Age" or displaced into outer space.

At the time that I taped these programs, I was not only shocked as a critic but as a parent. This is the imaginative universe that my two-and-one-half-year-old was soon to enter? Not if I could help it. However, that same spring, *Parent's Magazine* carried an article by past editor Phyllis La Farge, *Learning to Live With the Bomb*, in which she argued against the wishful protectionism of parents who "try to encourage hopefulness by keeping silent about nuclear weapons, the arms race, and other issues." [1]

La Farge points out that not only is such shielding impossible in the television era but that it leaves the child ill-prepared for adult citizenship. As she concludes, "In our times, I believe that true protection must take a different form than silence: raising children who will be able and willing to think about complex issues, make value judgments about the policies of their leaders, and act or vote on the basis of their judgments." [2]

The La Farge essay made me think. I regularly push my 18-to-60-year-old students to form their own definition of, and action in, what we commonly believe to be a participatory democracy. I say "push" because many of us as adults feel unable to participate in a meaningful sense; we feel powerless. I think now that such political alienation may have its roots in a post-WWII, nuclear-inspired protectionism of children that leaves them ill-equipped for adult participation. Two-and-one-half-year-olds quickly become eighteen-year-old voters. *If they do vote*, it may be a vote shaped more by the universe of children's television—allowed or surreptitious—than by parental discussion, passage of values and sense of empowerment.

That there is a real need for parent-child sharing and discussion of children's television is evident in a more subtle yet sustained aspect of the cartoon world—that of anti-Soviet propaganda. On the surface, the universe of children's commercial programming seems one of "we-they," the "we" being middle-class American society and the "they" being anyone else, and automatically "lesser," if not evil, by virtue of their difference from us. Yet, a closer look reveals more than simple ethnocentrism. On *Rocky-and-Bullwinkle*, for example, the evil threat lies in the action of Boris and Natasha, who are often the child's first, and for a long time only, undisguised introduction to "THE RUSSIANS."

Similarly, Brutus on *Popeye* goes much further. Consider the episode titled "Home, Sweet Home" which was a part of my random taping. In this episode, Popeye builds a home, only to have it destroyed by termites. The episode is one long contest between the termites and Popeye, who eventually "wins" by building his home (from frame to his pipe) out of steel and concrete. Here we have not only the image of life in a bomb shelter as a solution, *but* the termites, caricatures of gluttony and destruction, are stereotypically Asian and Slavic in physical appearance. Such characterizations explicitly teach children that the cultural bogeyman is not faceless but identifiable "red"—Chinese if not Russian.

The world of nuclear proliferation and other violent expressions is a world predicated upon a belief in "the enemy." If we wish to change this world, we need to not only face our knowledge of and fears about violence but to confront and think critically about the beliefs we hold and pass on to our children. Is mankind essentially contentious, competitive, destructive—making anyone different from us an enemy? Or is mankind a species of great variation, with much to share and even more to gain from cooperation?

If the second suggestion seems "nice but naive, idealistic," might it be because *we* grew up on television that made the first suggestion its premise, and with parents themselves shocked by the atrocities of World War II, holocaust to the Bomb, and hence unable to offer to us a critical sense of possibility?

In the immediate period of Soviet "glasnost," we might work as well towards such openness—as individuals confronting our own heritage so we can then help our children, as parents and teachers, to live with a sense of a realizable future. This would allow us to see commercial children's television not solely as a threatening universe but as one of possibility—a necessary arena for children to come to terms with late twentieth century America, a forum for exploration and discussion toward peace.

Notes:

1. Phyllis La Farge, "Learning to Live With the Bomb," *Parents Magazine* (March 1987) p.214.

2. La Farge, 215.

CELEBRATIONS OF PEACE

Thoughts on Ceremonies

by Susan Hopkins

Viki Diamond, a wonderful folksinger and storyteller from New York, shares with us these very important thoughts to keep in mind as we enter this section of peace education: "I don't see 'peace' as a developmentally appropriate concept for young children. Pre-schoolers need language development toward conflict management and so do their parents in relation to their children. They need the language and sensitivity toward unsnarling conflict far more than they need understanding of it."

Keeping Viki's thoughts in mind about the appropriateness of teaching "peace" to young children, perhaps one way to help them start comprehending some of the concepts involved in "peace" is to have a ceremony—a dignified celebration—based on the concept of caring about others.

We have enjoyed some very special, very dignified, and very meaningful ceremonies with peace being the cornerstone. The preparations have been the basis of curriculum for days preceding, allowing the day of celebration to be met with more awareness and anticipation.

Following is a description of two ceremonies, the Candle Lighting Ceremony and the Peace Day Celebration, which have been quite special for the children, their families, and staff. Care must be taken, as Viki points out, to keep concepts concrete for young children. Peace is very abstract, so we must involve the children in activities which include caring about others, expressing feelings, and problem-solving. Children need to learn about peace through participation in real activities such as sending messages of friendship to people near and far, verbalizing their feelings in a great variety of situations, and working through problems by negotiation with others.

The following letter was sent to the parents of our 4-year-olds at the university during the week of the Summit Meeting in November 1985. It describes our efforts towards peace with young children. They were very impressed by the candle and the moment after lighting it in which we were all silent.

Dear Sunshine Parents:

As you are well aware, today marks the advent of the American-Soviet summit conference—our hopes for world peace rest in the hands of these leaders and the decisions they will be making.

We feel this important time should be recognized and used as an opportunity for discussions of peace with the Sunshine children. It's never too early to begin developing this concept which is crucial to our very existence. Therefore, this week we will be doing several things to help the children relate on a personal level to the importance of managing conflicts in a peaceful way:

1. We will discuss the "news" that our President and the Soviet Chairman are talking together to try to find ways to solve problems without fighting.

2. We will light a candle and put it in the office on Tuesday to symbolize our hopes for successful talks. "Better to light a candle than curse the darkness."

3. It will be suggested to the children that they might want to ask you to light a candle at home and put it in the window to show your support for world peace.

4. We will act out several children's conflicts and problem–solve resolutions using words rather than aggression. We will work on these role–playing dramas for several days with the children who will gradually take more and more of the roles and the leadership.

We hope these activities will have meaning to every child in relationship to their own lives and the importance of peaceful conflict management. If you have any concerns or any feedback about how your child reacts to these activities, we would certainly appreciate hearing from you.

Susan/Kathy

Peace Day

International Peace Day, the day the United Nations General Assembly convenes in mid-September, has also become a tradition at our school. Several months ahead of time we obtain a weather balloon and curriculum ideas from:

Paul Portner
c/o Riverdale Elementary School
13222 Lewis St.
Garden Grove, CA 92643

Especially successful activities have included:

—Decorating the balloon as the Earth.

—Drawing pictures and dictating messages of peace on small paper plates which are tied together for a "tail" on the balloon.

—Making banners by children and teachers to decorate around the "lift-off" area.

—Practicing "peace songs."

—Making "peace candles" from tissue rolls, glitter, and red paper.

The day of our celebration for peace (usually mid-September) is very special as children, families, and teachers gather in the designated area. The huge helium tank is wheeled in, the children gather round in a circle holding hands and singing, as the balloon is inflated. When time to launch it arrives, everyone is very quiet and a teacher shares a few special thoughts. Then the balloon is set off to share our message of peace. The children watch in awe. When the balloon can no longer be seen, we walk quietly past the Peace Candle which has been burning all day in the office. The celebration has much meaning for the children as they comment on it throughout the year.

An additional thought—your local newspaper might be willing to cover your "Peace Day Celebration."

Note: Since our last celebration of International Peace Day, we have learned of the environmental concern that the balloon could land in the ocean, causing pollution. In the future we will reconsider the use of this type of balloon as part of our celebration.

PEACE (poem)

by Carol A. Clark

Engulfing hugs from small arms
Giving love, secure in its return.
Sunshine faces glowing with anticipation,
Concentrating on restraining, if only for a moment,
The explosive energy contained within.

The candle flame flickers, our symbol of peace.
My child, and yours, stare wonderingly.
The purity of flame reflecting
The innocence and hope of the child.

I stare, wonderingly, at each child
Haloed by unshed tears.
Facing the future in the children,
I stoop to shoulder the burden of love:
The unending quest for peace.

<u>Songs of Celebration</u>

WE'VE GOT THE WHOLE WORLD IN OUR HANDS
(Traditional)

1) We've got the whole world in our hands (repeat 3 times, 4th time slowly)

2) I've got my mother and my father in my hands (repeat 3 times)
We've got the whole world in our hands

3) I've got you and me brother in my hands (repeat 3 times)
We've got the whole world in our hands

4) I've got you and me sister in my hands (repeat 3 times)
We've got the whole world in our hands

5) I've got the little bitty baby in my hands (repeat 3 times)
We've got the whole world in our hands

6) I've got my friends in (Nicaragua, Russia, etc.) in my hands

Adapted from "He's Got the Whole World in His Hands," *Best Loved Songs of the American People*, p. 370, Denes Agay, Doubleday, Gordon City, N.Y., 1975

MAY THERE ALWAYS BE SUNSHINE
(Russian children's song)

May there always be sunshine
May there always be blue sky
May there always be Mama
May there always be me.

Poost vsegda boodyet solntse
Poost vsegda boodyet nyeba
Poost vsegda boodyet mama
Poost vsegda boodoo ya.

"May There Always Be Sunshine"
Original Words by Lav Oshanin
Music by Arkadi Ostrovsky
©Copyright 1964 by MCA Music Canada, A Division of MCA Canada LTD., Willodale, Ontario. Rights administered by MCA Music Publishing, A Division of MCA, Inc., New York, NY 10019 for USA.
Used by permission

THIS LITTLE LIGHT OF MINE
(Traditional)

This little light of mine, I'm gonna let it shine;

This little light of mine, I'm gonna let it shine;

This little light of mine, I'm gonna let it shine;

Let it shine, let it shine, let it shine.

Additional songs may be found in *Rise Up Singing*, edited by Peter Blood-Patterson, a Sing Out publication.

IF YOU'RE HAPPY AND YOU KNOW IT
(Traditional)

If you're happy and you know it, clap your hands;
If you're happy and you know it, clap your hands;
If you're happy and you know it, then your face will surely show it,
If you're happy and you know it, clap your hands.

If you're sad and you know it, give a cry.

If you're angry and you know it, give a growl.

If you're peaceful and you know it, touch a friend.

If you're happy and you know it, shout "Hurray!"

CLAP HANDS AND SHOUT HURRAY
(To the tune of "The Farmer in the Dell")

For_____(child's name)_____is here today; (repeat)

Look around and find a friend who came to school today.

SPECIAL CALENDAR DAYS

Celebrate Earth Day!

Earth day is an opportunity to celebrate and cherish our planet. Prior to the Earth Day Celebration we can be participating in many activities with young children which help promote environmental awareness, appreciation, and preservation. These activities can be very experiential and concrete—therefore appropriate for even the youngest of children. Good early childhood education practice suggests that we take cues from the children in order to expand their learning. Young children are wonderful observers and appreciators of the natural environment. By paying close attention to their questions, observations, and interests we can help them grow in their understanding of how to love and take care of the Earth. Following are a few ideas which are appropriate for all ages, and certainly work well with the youngest.

Activities to Build Awareness and Appreciation

Observation is an important skill in learning to preserve our environment. Activities could include:

1. Get to know a tree. Select a tree. Look at it from a distance. Trace its shape with your finger. Describe its shape with words.
   • Hold out your arms to show how the branches grow.
   • Get closer to your tree. What is the bark like? What are the leaves like?
   • How are you and your tree alike? How are you different?

2. Mini-forest.
   • Lic on the lawn, face down. Spread the grass apart and describe what you see—plants, animals, insects, etc.
   • If there were no grass, how would the mini-forest be different?

3. Touch and feel hike.
   • Find the hairiest leaf around.
   • Find the smoothest rock around.
   • Find the softest leaf around.
   • Find the roughest twig around.
   • Find something cool/warm.
   • Find something dry/wet.
   • Find something bumpy.

Stories can help children develop appreciation of our environment too. There are many, but here are a few of special value:
   Baylor Byrd, *I'm in Charge of Celebrations*
   Cooney, Barbara, *Miss Rumphius*
   Romanova, Natalia, *Once There Was a Tree*

Community-building activities such as the creation of a hiking club, an ecology club, a nature club—whatever interests you—help members support one another and grow together. Clubs can be wonderful for family involvement.

Activities for Empowerment

With adult encouragement, children can and must be empowered to start taking responsibility in age-appropriate preservation activities.

   • Plant a garden using soil from your compost pile.

   • Learn about power and energy—electricity, water, fire, air—and practice conservation measures.

- Gather litter in your neighborhood and make a poster to encourage people to clean up their litter.

- Recycle aluminum, paper, plastic (and anything else which is safe for children to handle) and use the money earned for a special project. (This is a good family activity.)

- Develop a project to help the environment, such as tree planting, helping to save an endangered species, or oil-spill cleanup. Learn about the problem with the children. Find out what is needed to help and take any local action if possible. Sources of information include Sierra Club, Tree Society, local environmental groups, and even your newspaper. For long distance projects money can be earned with the children through bake sales, stationary-making and sales, and/or recycling. Letters dictated by the children expressing their feelings and concerns can be written to local newspapers, legislators, or environmental groups.

Activities for Celebration

Celebrate Earth Day with children and families. Activities may include:

- A picnic to acknowledge your accomplishments in helping to preserve our environment.

- A hike to a special local area.

- A potluck with songs, cooperative games, and merriment.

Environmental education is an opportunity for teachers and families to all come together to work actively with the children while giving them real experiences in appreciating and preserving the world. These opportunities for children's best growth must not be missed, neither for the future citizens of our planet nor for Mother Earth!

Activities Calendar: Celebrations, Festivals, and Holidays Around the World

Contributions by Viann Sanders, Kathy Barnett, and Orange County Educators for Social Responsibility

Note: You will want to read several months ahead in the following calendars so that you can order supplemental materials suggested, thus allowing time for their arrival.

All people enjoy celebrating. Celebrations are only one part of a culture, but are important as they symbolize aspects of the culture which the people value. As we learn about these celebrations we are provided with an opportunity to discover, with children, some of the special values and traditions in people's lives all over the world. Remember, however, it is important that we learn not only about celebrations, but also about people's daily lives as the daily life of a people is the real culture.

Listed below are holidays and special occasions that relate to children, family, culture, or nature. This is not a conclusive list of events, only a representation of what is happening around the world. Many holidays are celebrated in several countries and it would be interesting to compare celebrations if you are working with older children. For example, Festivals of Light are celebrated in countries such as Sweden, India, and the United States in December. Children's Days are celebrated in Japan and Turkey. Some of these dates may change according to the calendar.

January

January 1—Oshogatsu, Japanese New Year. Many Japanese start the New Year fresh by cleaning the house, saying thanks for the past year, and wishing for a happy new year. Traditional foods are served at this time. To observe Japanese New Year children could help clean the home or classroom and then prepare and eat osechi ryori (boiled vegetables).

January 15—Birthday of Martin Luther King, Jr., a famous American civil rights leader and winner of the 1964 Nobel Peace Prize. He is perhaps best remembered for his stirring speech in which he repeated his dream for a future that held peace, justice, and equality for all Americans. Ask children, "What do you think the future will hold?" Have them write or draw about it.

January 16—National Nothing Day

January 18—A.A. Milne born 1882. Read some *Winnie the Pooh* stories and/or poems; look for the subtle humor even older children will appreciate!

January 20—First official basketball game played in Springfield, Mass., 1892. Also, after 444 days, 52 American hostages were released from Iran in 1981.

January 27—Vietnam Peace Treaty, 1973.

January 31—First U.S. satellite launched, 1958.

Mid-January to mid-February—China. Chinese New Year. At this time of year, red paper is placed on window sills and doors to bring good luck. When children walk around their neighborhood singing, they are often given gifts of rice cakes and oranges. Fireworks are also an important part of the New Year's festivities. This celebration includes several special occasions. The Ching Sen is a time set aside to show respect for ancestors. A dragon made with brightly colored paper is the highlight of the Parade of Dragons. The dragons are a symbol of goodness and strength. This holiday opens up the opportunity to learn about a Chinese festival, make lanterns, or decorate a box to look like a dragon and have a parade. Children could also learn about their own ancestors and family history.

End of January to beginning of February—Viet Nam. Tet (New Year). Many homes decorate with a leafy branch covered with fruit and flowers to bring a happy and prosperous new year. The entrances to some homes and businesses may have bamboo poles decorated with colored paper, bells, leaves, and lanterns. It would be fun to decorate home or school with paper flowers, bells, etc. in honor of Tet.

February

February 1—National Freedom Day. Give children this list of names of eight people who fought for freedom in different ways and for different groups of people, and let them find out a little about each one. Martin Luther King, Jr., Susan B. Anthony, Helen Keller, A.S. Neill, Isadora Duncan, Walt Whitman, Mohandas Gandhi, and Scott Nearing.

February 7—Beatles begin first U.S. tour, 1964. Expose children to old Beatles music and memorabilia if possible; discuss their music and its effect on music today!

February 9—Haiti. Carnival Lamayote. One of the children's activities is to decorate cardboard boxes, called lamayotes. Inside the boxes they put a surprise that people are supposed to guess. Many of the children also dress in costumes. Use a guessing box for a sensory experience along with a discussion of Haiti.

February 11—National Inventor's Day. The Wizard of Menlo Park, Thomas Edison, was born on this day in 1847. When he was only 10 years old, he set up a real laboratory in his father's basement. Later on in his life, he invented the light bulb, the phonograph, the movie projector, and the mimeograph. No wonder National Inventor's Day is celebrated on his birthday!

February 12—Abraham Lincoln's Birthday. Read and discuss the Gettysburg Address with your students.

February 14—Denmark. Fjortende Februar (Fourteenth of February). Children exchange silly notes and pressed snowdrops (flowers) as a symbol of friendship. The notes are not signed and it is part of the fun guessing from whom they come. For variety celebrate Valentine's Day in this manner.

February 15—Susan B. Anthony's Birthday. Anthony was a suffragette who worked hard for women's rights, especially the right to vote. (The word suffrage means the right to vote.) She died before women were granted the vote in 1920, but she made a famous prediction: "Failure is impossible."

February 20—Brotherhood Week Celebration (Always includes Washington's birthday).

February 22—Friendship Week (week of Washington's birthday). This is a great week to think about friends. Have your children write essays or poems on "What is a friend?" They might enjoy reading the Peanuts book, *A Friend Is*, drawing pictures of their best friends, or writing letters to their friends telling them why they are so important.

February 23—Take a Bath Day. In 1851 President Millard Fillmore put the first bathtub in the White House.

February 25—Bank Your Money Day. The first savings bank was opened in North America, 1819.

February 28—Nijinsky's Birthday. Vaslav Nijinsky was probably the greatest male dancer in the history of ballet. He was so strong he could leap across the entire stage in a single bound. He was born in Russia in 1890 and trained there. Celebrate his birthday with some stretching and leaping exercises.

March

March—Women's History Month. Send $1.00, for an illustrated catalog listing materials available on the subject, to National Women's History Project, Box 3726, Santa Rosa, California 95402, or call (707) 526-5974.

March 2—Pyramid Day. On March 2, 1818, three famous pyramids near Giza in Egypt were opened. The Great Pyramid is 450 feet (almost as tall as a 50-story building). Research how and why these elaborate tombs were built 4,000 years ago.

March 3—Doll's Day in Japan. In Japan, doll making is a fine art, and dolls can be family heirlooms that are passed from generation to generation. Each March 3 these special dolls are displayed on red cloth-covered steps covered with peach blossoms. The day is called Hina Matsuri, the Doll Festival. You can celebrate this special day by having children bring a special doll for a class display, and having a tea party, with everyone sitting on the floor. Children may paint pictures of peach blossoms by using cotton balls as the brush for the flower.

March 8—Harriet Tubman Day. Born in about 1820 Harriet Tubman was the great African-American woman who led more than 300 slaves to freedom before the Civil War, and worked for women's rights and suffrage till her death in 1913.

March 16—Rocket Shot Day. Dr. Robert Goddard, an American scientist, worked on figuring out how to send a ship into space from the time he was 16 years old. On March 16, 1926, he, along with his wife and 2 assistants, went to his Aunt Effie's farm near Auburn, Massachusetts. There the first liquid-fuel rocket in history was fired. It was less than 12 feet high, including the launching pad! Fun idea: Have children construct a fantastic space rocket from scrap materials.

March 19—St. Joseph's Day. This is a great holiday in Italy where they hold elaborate feasts with abundant food and flowers. Hold a classroom Italian banquet on the eve (18th) with pasta, Italian flags, music, etc. (In California, remember March 19th is the day the swallows return to San Juan Capistrano. Brave the crowds for the festivities, if you dare!)

March 20—First day of Spring. Day and night are equal all over the world. Scientists call this the vernal equinox. People of Afghanistan, Iran and the Bahai faith celebrate their new year tonight and tomorrow. It is called Nowuz. Celebrants take special spring baths, scrub their homes, wear new clothes, and visit friends. The traditional feast is made up of seven foods that begin with the Persian letter "S." They represent the seven archangels of God in the Zoroastrian religion. With these countries in the news so much, see if there is any coverage of this event, or hold another feast with seven "S" foods.

March 21—Albert Einstein's Birthday, 1879, in Ulm, Germany. He received the Nobel prize in physics in 1921. He was Jewish and a strong believer in Zionism. The Nazis burned his books. In 1940 he became an American citizen. His theories established a new concept of the physical world and led to such advances as harnessing atomic energy. Have students research his life, and have older students discuss the meaning behind the following quotes of Einstein: "The unleashed power of the atom has changed everything save our modes of thinking and we thus drift toward unparalleled catastrophe." "There is no scientific antidote (to the atomic bomb), only education. You've got to change the way people think."

March 21—Egypt. Sham al-Nessim. On this day the whole family goes on a picnic to enjoy the wonders and smells of spring. Together they pick the best spot for the picnic. After a specially prepared lunch, the family plays games, flies kites, sings, tells stories, or goes for a ride on the Nile. A greeting used on this day is "al Salamu Alaycum" which means "Peace be with you." A class or family could have their own Sham al-Nessim holiday by planning and preparing all the necessary parts for a successful picnic.

March 22—Marcel Marceau's Birthday. Marcel Marceau is the world's best-known mime, an actor who expresses himself only with movement, no words. He was born in France and loved pantomime as a child. He carefully watched the movements of people and animals, and loved the movies of Charlie Chaplin and others. As a young man he studied mime with a famous teacher, and then created his most famous character, Bip. Have children, alone or in small groups, do pantomimes. You can give them ideas to start with, and later they can use their own ideas.

March 24—March Museum Day. The National Gallery of Art in Washington, D.C. was established by Congress on March 4, 1937. It truly belongs to the citizens of America, and since opening in 1941, millions of people have attended it and enjoyed its wonderful collection of paintings and sculpture. Take a field trip to a museum, if possible. Set up a museum in your classroom or home.

March 25—Greek Independence Day. The Greek flag was adopted in 1822 while their war of independence from Turkish rule was being fought. For more information about Greece, write: Press and Information Service of Greece, 601 Fifth Avenue, New York, NY 10022.

March 30—Vincent Van Gogh's Birthday, 1853. Some of his most famous paintings are self-portraits. Our Cultural awareness is enriched through the study of art. Have children sit in front of a mirror and do self-portraits.

March 31—Cesar Chavez' Birthday. Have students research migrant farm workers in California.

March and April.—India. Holi. During this harvest and spring celebration, children in India squirt colored water on each other. Water play would be a way to introduce this holiday.

April

April—Pets Are Wonderful Month. Develop a mini unit on proper care of pets.

April 2—International Children's Book Day. Libraries all over the world are buzzing with activity today. Many special programs and exhibits are happening as they celebrate International Children's Book Day. April 2 was selected because it is Hans Christian Andersen's birthday. Have children make their own personalized book plates.

April 7—World Health Day. W.H.O. stands for World Health Organization, an agency of the United Nations. Its purpose is to build a world of healthier people.

April 8—(Gautama) Buddha's Birthday, around 621 B.C. in India. In 592 B.C. he became a full Buddha, one who is the "Enlightened," and has attained the highest degree of knowledge possible for man in this solar system. His birthday is celebrated in Japan as Hana Matsuri (The Flower Festival). Legend says that when Buddha was born, flower petals fell from the sky. Make tissue paper flowers and string them together to make garlands to decorate windows, doors, etc.

April 15—Income Tax Day. Find out how much of each tax dollar goes for health, education, welfare, transportation, defense, etc. See page 17 of the April, 1985, NEA TODAY as a start.

April 22—Earth Day. See beginning of this section for suggested activities.

April 22—United States. Arbor Day. (Date may change according to the state.) In 1872, J. Sterling Morton persuaded Nebraska to plant trees in barren areas. Now on his birthday, many places encourage people to plant trees. This could be a time to plant trees at your school or in your neighborhood. Money could be earned to purchase a tree by recycling newspapers. People like John Chapman (Johnny Appleseed) and George Washington Carver might be mentioned for their contributions to nature.

April 23—Turkey. Children's Day. Celebrates the importance of children to the future. Many businesses offer free gifts to children such as ice cream and movie tickets. Some children practice doing official jobs. A class might visit their school offices to learn more about how the school operates.

April 26—John Audubon's Birthday. American artist and naturalist was born over 200 years ago. Take children on a bird watching field trip around the school or neighborhood.

Last week of April to the first week in May—Holland. Tulip Festival. Children learn about Holland including the tulips, wooden shoes (klompen), and the native costumes, as well as Dutch cheeses.

May

May 1—England. May Day. After decorating the maypole, children sing and dance around it. Children make their own maypole and learn dances and songs relating to spring. To celebrate spring many other countries have special traditions on this day.
Belguim: Celebrates May Day with parades and fairs.
France: The flower, lily of the valley, is the center of May Day festivities. The flowers are picked, worn, and given as gifts.
Hawaii: Lei Day. Everyone wears flower leis.

May 3—Sun Day. A day set aside to make people aware of solar energy uses. Try a few of the activities described in *Catch a Sunbeam*, a book of solar study and experiments published by Harcourt Brace Jovanovich. A good day to plant a sunflower.

May 5—Feast of Flags, or Kodomo-no-hi. This is Children's Day in Japan. Tall poles are set up near Japanese houses and red and black flags in the shape of fish are flown from them. There is one flag for each boy in the family. This holiday used to be called Boy's Day. Now that it is called Children's Day, families will probably fly flags for girls, too! Have your children make banners for themselves, using their initials for decorations.

May 8—Mother's Day—Have children interview their mothers: Where was she born; what year? What was her maiden name? What was she like as a girl?

May 12—Mary Ashton Rice Livermore was the first woman to exercise her right to write and report on this day in 1860. As an editor with the *New Covenant*, she covered the Chicago Republican National Convention where Abraham Lincoln was nominated for the presidency. Discuss the First Amendment's guarantee of freedom of speech and a newspaper's responsibility to report the facts as objectively as possible. Give your students first-hand experience by publishing your own paper.

May 13—Arthur Sullivan, of the musical team Gilbert and Sullivan, was born in 1842. Have children lipsync to a famous opera or operetta. This is excellent practice for foreign language students, and an abbreviated version of a comic opera can be turned into a fun skit. Children might also draw faces on their hands. When you put your index finger together with your thumb, it forms a circle that makes a perfect mouth. Draw eyes and nose above on the side of the index finger, and lips around the hole. Soon you'll have a whole chorus of altos and sopranos.

May 14—Robert Owen's Birthday, 1771, the 19th century proponent of the utopian society. He proposed a system of cooperative communities in which the work and the rewards would be equally shared by all. Discuss how you could apply these theories to the classroom. Ask students to imagine an ideal day. What would they wear? What would they do? What would they eat? Who, if anyone, would be in charge? You might even try it and then discuss the problems and how to deal with them.

May 15—The state of Israel was established on this day in 1948 after the United Nations partitioned Palestine. This represented the fulfillment of the Jewish people's belief in God's promise of their own holy land. Students are seeing the strife that is occurring in this area now. Introduce them to the Jewish people's dire need at that time and of the cause of the Palestine people's unrest. Introduce them to the geography and cultures of the Middle East and the security risks that contribute to the difficulties in achieving peace in the region. The UN Store has Middle East paper dolls that could be used with younger children.

May 15—Over the Rainbow Day. Born on this date in 1856 was L. Frank Baum, author of *The Wonderful Wizard of Oz*, which was published in 1900. He wrote 14 "Oz" books before his death in 1919. Since that time, other writers have taken us on these imaginary trips by continuing to write about "somewhere over the rainbow." Something fun to do is make rainbow sneakers (instead of ruby slippers!). Children can decorate their tennies (with permission from home) with permanent markers or acrylic paints. Also, any interested children can contact the International Wizard of Oz Club, Fred M. Meyer, Secretary, 220 N. 11th St., Escanaba, Michigan 49829. (Among other things, the club offers full-color maps of Oz.)

May 18—World Good Will Day. This day used to be called Peace Day. It is the anniversary of the opening of the first Hague Peace Conference held in 1899, when presenters from many countries came together in Holland to organize for better international relations and make laws to govern all nations. The United Nations now carries on the quest for peace which began then. Have children find peace symbols, such as the dove, the "V" for victory sign, and the circle with the bird tract that was so popular in the 60's. Maybe they can design some new, original ones.

May 23—Mary Cassatt's Birthday. She was an influential and famous Impressionist who concentrated on paintings of mothers and children and scenes of family life with sensitivity. Celebrate her birthday by having children make drawings or paintings from their family lives: suppertime, playing and working together, special family occasions.

May 25—Africa Freedom Day. On this day in 1963, the Organization of African Unity was founded, and the peoples of Africa in many places celebrate with speeches, parades, special sports events, and songfests. Teach children some words from the language spoken in the Congo, Lonkundo: peanut-nguba; bananas-mankondo; oranges-ilala; sweet potato-baenge; beans-babinsi; greens-banganju.

May 28—Sierra Club founded, 1892. Members of the Sierra Club are dedicated to clean air and water, wise land use, and energy conservation. Address for writing for brochures and information: Sierra Club, 530 Bush St., San Francisco, CA 94108. Another good address to have on file is the U.S. Environmental Protection Agency, Washington, D.C. 20460.

June

June 5—World Environment Day. On June 5, 1972, the U.N. held its conference on the Human Environment and proclaimed World Environment Day. Hold a litter cleanup race; give each participant one trash bag (or more). The idea is to pick up as much litter as you can from your school grounds or the neighborhood in a set amount of time, say, one-half hour.

June 6—Recycling Day. You can set up a center in your classroom or home. Decorate a large, empty box or crate. Have children contribute items such as shirt cardboard and empty cardboard tubes, empty containers, spools, egg cartons, empty jars, ribbons, greeting cards, etc. Use the items for art projects, robot making, etc.

June 15—Smile Power Day. This was started by Dr. Robert Gibson, a Hawaiian dentist. Here is a riddle you can try: (Q) When you give it to someone else, you're almost sure to get it back. What is it? (A) A smile. To get more information write: The Smilepower Institute, Suite 717, 1441 Kapiolani Boulevard, Honolulu, Hawaii 96814.

The weekend closest to the 24th—Sweden. Midsummer. The holiday marks the longest day of the year. It is celebrated in several Northern European countries (such as Finland and Norway). On this day in many areas the sun doesn't set. In Sweden, fresh green birch twigs are placed everywhere. A pole is decorated similar to the maypole. The people dress in native costumes and participate in traditional dances. The sun and its position to the earth might be discussed.

End of June—Turkey. Sheker Bairam. Candy Festival. Children eat candy called loukam (red or green gelatin covered with powdered sugar, similar to gumdrops). Children give gifts of bright colored handkerchiefs. A color sorting activity with gumdrops or beads is fun. Also for an art project the children may decorate their own handkerchiefs with fabric crayons or paints or design their own on a square of fabric.

July

First two weeks in July—Czechoslovakia. Stráznice Folklore Festival. During the festival the performers do traditional folk dances and songs. Here is an opportunity to teach some folk dances.

July 26 to August 31—Austria. Salzburg Festival. A huge celebration honoring Austrian classical music, operas, and orchestras. At this time the music of Johann Strauss (the "Blue Danube Waltz"), Ludwig Van Beethoven (many symphonies), and Wolfgang Amadeus Mozart ("The Marriage of Figaro" opera) could be introduced. While listening to some of the music, the children enjoy drawing or painting according to how the music makes them feel.

August

First week in August—Wales. Eisteddfod. Festivals and competitions honoring native music, poetry, literature, and drama. This provides an opportunity to learn about Wales and do lots of singing. One Welsh writer is Dylan Thomas.

The beginning of August—India. Raksh Bandhan. At this time a day is set aside for siblings to do special things for each other. At school children list their ideas about how they can be helpful to their brothers or sisters, or to other people.

Second week in August—Gallup, New Mexico. Inter-Tribal Indian Ceremonial. North American and Central American Indians come together to participate in sports, rodeos, and ceremonial dances. The festivities include an exhibit of Indian arts and crafts, judging of art work, an all-Indian parade, and food. Children can learn about Native American games, crafts, dances, and foods. (For information on the ceremonial call 800-242-4282.)

September

First Saturday in September—Scotland. Highland Games of Scotland. Many people will wear their native costumes such as kilts. During this festival there are bagpipe competitions, native highland dancing, and traditional sporting competitions. The sports events include throwing the caber (a tree trunk), and tug of war. Also celebrated in Nova Scotia, Canada.

September 7—National Grandparents' Day. Discuss and write stories and poems about grandparents, or make greeting cards for grandparents or older people children are close to.

September 8—International Literacy Day. A good day for children to learn 5 new words and teach them to their little brothers and sisters, or to their parents.

September 13—Artist Robert Indiana's Birthday, 1928. He designed the postage stamp in 1973 with the word "Love" on it. Have children design their own peaceful message stamps.

September 14—National Hispanic Heritage Week. Children may write to someone their age in a Spanish-speaking country. For information on how to get a pen pal, write to: International Friendship League, 22 Batterymarch, Boston, Massachusetts, 02109.

September 17—Citizenship Day. Children can register as a citizen of the world. Address: Planetary Citizens, 777 U.N. Plaza, New York, N.Y. 10017.

September 22—Pen Pal Day. Children can have pen pals from another country by sending a self-addressed stamped envelope for a registration form to: Pen Pals, 22 Batterymarch Street, Boston, Massachusetts 02109.

September __ (date varies)—Rosh Hashana, the Jewish New Year, began at sunset last night. Today Jews blow the shofar to welcome in the year. What is a shofar? It is a ram's horn that is hollow like a trumpet.

September 28—National Good Neighbor Day. Try to do a favor for your neighbor. Have children discuss or write about what being a good neighbor really means.

September 29—Sundown Dance Day. One of the most famous Native American celebrations is the sundown dance of the Taos Indians in New Mexico. Every year on this date Indians there perform traditional dances including the eagle dance, turtle dance, horsetail dance, and the toe heel. For this dance: Take a step with your right foot. Put your weight on only the ball of your foot (toe). Now, lower your right heel so your whole foot is on the ground (heel). Next, take a step with your left foot, and again put your weight only on the ball (toe). Last, lower your left heel (heel). A fun dance to teach children. Sources of information: Global Education Association, 552 Park Avenue, East Orange, N.J. 07017 and UN Center Global Gift Store, 2428 N. Grand, Santa Ana, CA (great for international gifts, cards, and educational items). You might also ask your children to make up their own version of what the eagle, turtle, and horsetail dances might look like.

End of September to beginning of October—Germany. Munchener Oktoberfest. A celebration centered around eating, drinking, fair attractions, and shopping. Parades, native costumes, and dances are also seen.

End of September to Beginning of October—Australia. Carnival of Flowers. The festivities include cultural events, sports, agricultural exhibits, and appreciation of the arts (such as music, theater, children's contributions, films, and crafts). The orchid is also important to this festival. Older children can learn that it is spring in Australia due to the Earth's relationship to the sun.

October

October 2—Gandhi's Birthday. Gandhi helped free India from British rule, not with guns and battles, but through his own method of nonviolence. The world came to know Gandhi and his peaceful methods of change. (Martin Luther King used Gandhi's ideas in his fight for civil rights.) Gandhi is known as Mahatma Gandhi, which means Great Soul. Fun to do—teach children the lotus position—Gandhi was a faithful practicer of yoga.

October 2—Universal Children's Day Celebration. This is a United Nations sponsored day, which fosters "world-wide fraternity and understanding among children." UNICEF, which sponsors this celebration, helps over 900 million children world-wide through health care, nutrition, and education. You can encourage children to raise money for UNICEF on Halloween and can get everything you need to "Trick or Treat for UNICEF" by writing to U.S. Committee for UNICEF, 331 E. 38th St., N.Y., N.Y., 10016. Ask for the item 1001 (UNICEF money collection carton).

October 4—St. Francis of Assisi's Feast. One of Christianity's most beloved saints, St. Francis loved all the world and cared deeply for animals as well as people. He once tamed a fierce wolf so the animal lived peacefully in the village of Gubbio, and was fed by the people there, who came to love him dearly. St. Francis is the patron saint of animals. Children could make bird feeders, such as stuffing a pine cone with peanut butter and corn meal mixture, and rolling it in bird seed to hang.

October 20—National Cleaner Air Week begins.

October 20—Clown Around Day. Barnum and Bailey Circus opened on this day in 1873.

October 21—In 1897, Thomas Edison turned on the first electric light—what would life be like without it?

October 24—United Nations Day. The U.N. Flag (a map of the Earth as it looks from above the North Pole) is a good project for students. The olive branches around the map of the Earth are ancient symbols of peace. Color the background of the flag sky blue, and leave the branches and map white. The U.N. was organized at the end of World War II as a way of preventing another World War. Today, 150 nations (representing 4 billion people) work together in the U.N. to preserve peace and benefit mankind.

Note: The United Nations Store, 2482 N. Grand, Santa Ana, CA is a super source of teaching ideas, supplies, etc.

October 25—Picasso's birthday. Show prints of his work and have children try their hands at collage.

October 31—United States. Halloween. Instead of trick or treating, some children collect money to give to the United Nations for the children of the World. Children often have a fundraiser (paper drive, collect cans, or do chores around the house) and then send the money to the United Nations. (See United Nations Chart.)

October—Hawaii. Aloha Week. Hoólaulea. This commemorates Hawaiian traditions, culture, and customs. Listening to Hawaiian music and learning about the ukulele would be interesting. (See charts on Hawaiian culture.)

October and November—India. Diwali. Festival of Lights. Homes light oil candles to impress Lakshmi, the goddess of prosperity and to celebrate the harvest. Flashlights could be arranged in different shapes and patterns to look at in the dark.

November

November—Mexico. Guadalajara Harvest Festival. The celebration includes events such as parades, dances, food, chili cook-off, Mexican art, crafts, and folklore. Children enjoy learning the Mexican Hat Dance.

November 2—Day of the Dead. A Mexican holiday. Many people believe the souls of their loved ones return to earth for a visit. People prepare picnics and flowers and take them to the family graves where there is much feasting and merriment. Children could make skeleton masks, or use macaroni and spaghetti to make skeletons on construction paper.

November 7—Revolution Day. This is the national holiday of the USSR. It is the anniversary of Russia's revolution of 1917. In every major Soviet city, especially Moscow, the streets are decorated with colored lights and people are gathered to watch long military parades. Many children hold bright balloons.

November 10—Vachel Lindsay's Birthday. Vachel Lindsay was one of America's amazing characters, a modern day Johnny Appleseed, who walked all over the country planting not seeds, but poems. He read his poems aloud, traded them for meals and lodging, and enchanted people everywhere with his jazz-like rhythms. He roamed the country for more than 20 years, giving his poems away. "There is more poetry in the distribution of verse than in the writing of it." Have your children write poems to give away as gifts. Read Lindsay's poems; your library will have them.

Third Saturday in November—Thailand. Elephant Round Up. During the gathering there are demonstrations of what elephants can do, elephant races, and a tug-of-war between people and an elephant. Children might describe what some of these events look like using their imaginations. Also an opportunity to learn more about elephants.

December

December 1—Advent Day (Advent means "coming"). Only 24 days 'til Christmas! Have children recycle old Christmas cards to make new cards, calendars, and gifts.

December 5—Walt Disney's Birthday (1901-1966). Have children make flip-books to simulate the first cartoons.

December 7—Pearl Harbor Day. Also Ratification Day. Delaware was the first to ratify the U.S. Constitution in 1787. Have children find out the names of the other 12 original 13 states.

December 9—First Christmas Seals for sale, in 1907. Have children design their own, and discuss the meaning of Christmas seals.

December 13—Sweden. Luciadagen. Saint Lucia's Day. This day is the shortest day in Sweden. To celebrate the upcoming reappearance of the sun and spring, the children dress up in white costumes. In the morning they go around the house waking up everyone and serving a traditional breakfast of buns shaped in an X, cookies and coffee. For a morning snack children enjoy making buns out of biscuit dough and dressing in white costumes.

December—Monte Carlo, Monaco. International Circus Festival. Performers and nonperformers from around the world get together to enjoy circus acts, experiences, and ideas. Children love to organize their own circus including the acts, music, and refreshments.

The end of December to January 5—Russia. Russian Winter Festival. Included in this festival are cultural events such as performing arts and winter activities like sledding, ice skating, and playing in the snow. Read the folktale *Snow Girl* to the children.

December 26—United States. Kwanzaa. Families of African descent celebrate by lighting one candle a day for seven days. The colors of Kwanzaa are red, green, and black. The underlying theme is unity, specifically family unity. Another theme is harvest. Kwanzaa is an optional observance to avoid Christmas-like commercialization.

RESOURCES

Bibliography compiled by Rosmarie Greiner and Susan Hopkins

<u>Books For Children</u>

Parents and teachers are encouraged to read the following books to themselves prior to using them with children in order to determine age and interest appropriateness.

<u>Self-Awareness</u>

Brenner, Barbara, *Bodies*, E.P. Dutton, New York, 1973.

de Paola, Tomie, *Oliver Button is a Sissy*, Harcourt, Jovanich & Brace, New York, 1979.

Hall, Marie, *Just Me*, Scholastic Books, 1965.

Leaf, M. *Story of Ferdinand*, Viking Press, New York, 1938.

Lionni, Leo, *Fish is Fish*, Pinwheel Books, 1974.

Mitchell, Edna Preston, *The Temper Tantrum Book*, Viking Press, 1969.

Ross, Dave, *A Book of Hugs*, Thomas Y. Crowell, New York, 1980.

Sharmat, Marjorie, *I'm Not Oscar's Friend Any More*,* E. P. Dutton & Co., New York, 1975.

Steig, William, *Sylvester and the Magic Pebble*, Scholastic Books. 1969.

Viorst, Judith, *Alexander and the Terrible, Horrible, No Good, Very Bad Day*, Atheneum, 1976.

Wagner, Jenny, *John Brown, Rose and the Midnight Cat,* Bradbury Press, Scarsdale, New York, 1977.

<u>Awareness of Self and Others</u>

Agestinelli, Maria, *On Wings of Love*, Collins Publishers, New York, 1979.

Asch, Frank and Vagin, Vladimir, *Here Comes the Cat!*, Scholastic, Inc., New York, 1989.

Bang, Molly, *The Paper Crane*, Greenwillow Books, New York, 1985.

Blos, Joan, *Old Henry*, William Morrow and Co., New York, 1987.

Byars, Betsy. *Go and Hush the Baby*. Viking Press, New York, 1971.

Cohen, Miriam,   *Will I Have A Friend?*, Collier Books, 1971.
                    Best Friends.

Crary, Elizabeth,   *I Can't Wait*; Parenting Press, 1982.
                       I Want to Play;
                       My Name is Not Dummy.

de Paola, Tomie, *Nana Upstairs and Nana Downstairs*. Puffin Books, 1981.

Hayes, Sarah, *Eat Up, Gemma*, Lothrop Lee and Shepard Books, New York, 1988.

Hoban, Russell and Lillian, *Best Friends for Frances*, Scholastic Books, 1968.

Jeffers, Susan, *Stopping By Woods on a Snowy Evening* (by Robert Frost), E.P. Dutton, 1978.

Jonas, Ann, *Holes and Peeks*, Greenwillow Books, New York, 1984.

Kesselman, Wendy, *Emma*, Harper and Row, 1980.

Lionni, Leo, *Frederick*, Pantheon Books, 1973.

Lionni, Leo, *Six Crows*, Alfred A. Knopf, 1988.

Maclachlan, Patricia, *Mama One, Mama Two*, Harper and Row Publishers, New York, 1982.

Martin, Bill, and Archambault, John, *Knots on a Counting Rope*, Henry Holt & Company, 1987.

Oxenbury, Helen, *All Fall Down*, Macmillan Publishing Co., New York, 1987.

Peterson, Jeanne Whitehouse, *I Have a Sister Who Is Deaf*, Harper and Row, Publishers, New York, 1977.

Piper, Watty, *The Little Engine That Could*, Platt and Munk, 1961.

Polland, Barbara Kay, *Feelings: Inside You and Out Loud, Too*, Celestial Arts, 1975.

Polland, Barbara Kay, *Decision, Decisions, Decisions*, Celestial Arts, 1976.

Quinlan, Patricia, *Planting Seeds*, Annick Press, Ltd., Toronto, Canada, 1988.

Raffi, *One Light, One Sun*, (from the series, Raffi Songs to Read), Crown Publishers, Inc., New York, 1988.

Reyner, B., *My Mother is the Most Beautiful Woman in the World*, Lothrop, Lee and Shepard, 1966.

Rice, Shawn, *The Garden of One*, Oxford University Press, 1987.

Scott, Ann H. *On Mother's Lap*, McGraw-Hill, 1972.

Simon, Norma, *Why Am I Different?*, Albert Whitman, 1976.

Tsutsui, Yoriko, *Anna's Secret Friend*, Puffin Books, Penguin Books, New York, 1986.

Turkle, Brinton, *Deep in the Forest*, E. P. Dutton, New York, 1976.

Waxman, Stephanie, *What is a Girl? What is a Boy?*, Peace Press, 1976.

Wiethorn, Randall, *Rock Finds a Friend*, Green Tiger Press, San Diego, CA, 1988.

Williams, Linda, *The Little Old Lady Who Was Not Afraid of Anything*, Harper and Row, Publishers, New York, 1988.

Williams, Vera, *A Chair for My Mother*, Mulberry Books, New York, 1982.

Wittman, Sally, *A Special Trade*, Scholastic Books, 1978.

Zolotow, Charlotte, *Mr. Rabbit and the Lovely Present*, Harper and Row, 1974.

Conflict Management

Burningham, John, *Mr. Gumpy's Motor Car*, Thomas Y. Cronwell, 1973.
Mr. Gumpy's Outing, Holt, Rinehart and Winston, 1970.

de Paola, Tomie, *The Hunter and the Animals*, Holiday House, 1981.

de Paola, Tomie, *The Knight and the Dragon*, G.P. Putnam & Sons, 1980.

de Paola, Tomie, *The Legend of Blue Bonnet*, G.P. Putnam & Sons, 1983.

Feelings, Muriel, *Moja Means One*, Dial Press, 1971.
Jambo Means Hello, 1974.

Fitzhugh, Loise and Sandra Scoppetone, *Bang, Bang You're Dead*, Harper, 1969.

Global Awareness

Aardema, Verna, *Why Mosquitoes Buzz in People's Ears*, A West African Tale, The Dial Press, 1975.

Baylor, Byrd, *When Clay Sings*, Charles Scribner's Sons, 1972.

Bonruici, Peter, *The Festival*, Carolrhoda Books, Inc.

Crowder, Jack, *Tonibah and the Rainbow*, Upper Strata Ink, Bernalilla, New Mexico, 1986.

Demi, *Liang and the Magic Paintbrush,* Holt, Rinehart and Winston, 1980.

Garaway, Margaret K., *The Old Hogan*, Mesa Verde Press, Cortez, Colorado, 1986.

George, Chief Dan, *My Heart Soars*, Hancock Publishing, Toronto, 1974.

Goble, Paul, *The Girl Who Loved Wild Horses*, Bradbury Press, 1978.

Griego, Buchs and Gilbert, Kimball, *Tortillitas Para Mama*, Henry Holt and Company, New York, 1981.

Hilgartner, Carol and Metzger, Barbara, *Martin Luther King, Jr.—A Biography for Young Children*, order from: RAEYC, Box 356, Henrietta, New York, 14467 ($4.95 ea.).

Hoban, Russell, *A Bargain for Frances*, Scholastic Books.

Kotzwinkle, William, *The Return of Crazy Horse*, Farrar, Straus, and Giroux, New York, 1971.

Levinson, Riki, *Our Home is the Sea*, E. P. Dutton, New York, 1988.

Lionni, Leo, *Swimmy*, Scholastic Books, 1968.

Lobel, Anita, *Potatoes, Potatoes,** Harper, 1967.

Marshall, James, *George and Martha: Tons of Fun*, Houghton Mifflin & Co., Boston, 1980.

McDermott, Gerald, *Arrow to the Sun*, Puffin, 1981.
Anansi the Spider, Holt, Rinehart, & Winston, 1972.

Meyer, Linda D., *Harriet Tubman: They Called Me Moses*, Parenting Press, Inc. Seattle, Washington, 1988.

Morris, Ann, *Bread, Bread, Bread*, Lothrop, Lee and Shepard Books, New York, 1989.

Polacco, Patricia, *The Keeping Quilt*, Simon and Schuster, Inc., New York, 1988.

Politi, Leo, *Three Stalks of Corn*, Scribner, 1976.
*Pedro, the Angel of Olvera Street**, 1946.
The Nicest Gift, 1973.

Provensen, A. and M. A., *A Peaceable Kingdom: The Shaker Abecedarius*, Viking Press, New York, 1978.

Rice Bowers, Kathleen, *At This Very Minute*, Little, Brown and Co., 1983.

Rose, Anne, *Akimba and the Magic Cow,** Scholastic Books, 1976.

Seeger, Pete, and Hays, Michael, *Abiyoyo*, Macmillan, 1986. Tape narrated by James Earl Jones available from Scholastic.

Siberell, Anne, *Whale in the Sky*, E. P. Dutton, New York, 1982.

Spier, Peter, *People*, Doubleday and Co., 1980.

Steadman, Ralph, *The Bridge,** William Collins and World Publishing Co., 1972.

Steig, William, *Amos and Boris*, Farrar, Strauss and Giroux, 1971.

Takeshita and Suzuki, *The Park Bench*, Kane/Miller Book Publishers, Brooklyn, New York, 1988.

Udry, Janice, *Let's Be Enemies*, Harper and Row, 1961.

Wahl, Jan, *The Animals Peace Day*,* Crown Publishers, New York, 1970.

Winter, Jeanette, *Follow the Drinking Gourd*, Alfred A. Knopf, New York, 1988.

Zolotow, Charlotte,   *The Hating Book*, Harper and Row, New York, 1969
The Quarreling Book, Harper and Row, 1963
The Unfriendly Book,* Harper and Row, 1975.

Environments—Love of Nature

Ayres, Pam, *When Dad Cuts Down the Chestnut Tree*, Discovery Toys, Pleasant Hill, CA, 1988.

Bancroft, Henrietta, *Animals in Winter*,* Scholastic Books, 1963.

Baylor, Byrd, *I'm In Charge of Celebrations*, Charles Scribner's Sons, 1986.

Baylor, Byrd, *The Way to Start a Day*, Charles Scribner, New York, 1978.

Broger, Achim, *The Caterpillar's Story*,* Scroll Press, 1973.

Brown, Margaret Wise and Jeffers, Susan, *Baby Animals*, Random House, New York, Text, 1941, Illustrations, 1989.

Cavagnaro, David, and Cavagnaro, Maggie, *The Pumpkin People*,* Sierra Club Books, 1979.

Cooney, Barbara, *Miss Rumphius*, Viking, New York, 1982.

Cork, Barbara, *Mysteries and Marvels of Plant Life*, Usborne Publishing, Ltd., 1983.

Cox, Rosemund and Cork, Barbara, *Birds: Usborne First Nature*, EDC Publishing, 1980.

de Paola, Tomie, *Charlie Needs a Cloak*, Scholastic Book Services.

Hall, Marie, *Play with Me*, Viking Press, 1955.

Heller, Ruth,   *Chickens Aren't The Only Ones,* Grosset & Dunlap, 1985.
Animals Born Alive and Well, 1982.
The Reason for a Flower, 1983.

Heller, Ruth, *How to Hide a Butterfly and Other Insects*, Grosset & Dunlap, 1981.

Hoberman, Mary Ann, *A House is a House for Me*, Puffin Books, 1982.

Jordan, Helene, *How a Seed Grows*, Crowell, 1960.

Kilpatrick, Cathy, *Creepy Crawlers—Insects and Other Tiny Animals*, Usborne First Nature, EDC Publishers, 1982.

Krauss, Ruth, *The Carrot Seed*, Harper and Row, 1945.

Mitchell, Robert T., and Zim, Herbert S., *Butterflies and Moths: A Guide to the More Common American Species*, Golden Press, 1977.

Rice, Shawn, *The Garden of One*, Oxford University Press, New York, 1987.

Romanova, Natalia, *Once There Was a Tree*, Dial Books, 1985.

Scheffler, Ursel, *A Walk in the Rain*, G.P. Putnam's Sons, 1984.

Selsam, Millicent, and Ronald Goar, *Backyard Insects*, Scholastic
also many other books by Millicent Selsam concerning nature.

Selsam, *Seeds and More Seeds*,* 1959.

Shuttlesworth, *The Hidden Magic of Seeds*,* Rodale Press, 1976.

Snulevitz, Uri, *Dawn*, Farrar, Strauss, and Giroux, 1974.

Yolen, Jane, *Owl Moon*, Philomel Books, 1987.

Zion, Gene, *The Plant Sitter*, Trophy Books, 1959.

* indicates book is possibly out of print. These books can often be found at public libraries.

<u>Music Resources for Children</u>

<u>Tapes</u>

Chiqui, Chiqui, Chiqui, by Lisa Monet, from
Circle Sound Productions
P.O. Box 966
Arcata, CA 95521

Cloud Journeys
Won't You Be My Friend?
Berman/Barlin Dance a Story, Sing a Song
B & B Records
570 N. Arden
Los Angeles, CA 90004

Hello Everybody, by Rachel Buchman, from :
A Gentle Wind
P.O. Box 3103
Albany, N.Y. 12203
(518) 482-9023

Learning Through Movement, by Anne and Paul Barlin,
The Ward Ritchie Press.

Music for Little People (catalog), includes Raffi, Peter Alsop, and others.
1(800) 346-4445

Sally Rogers—Folksinger of peace songs, Record available from her:
P.O. Box 111
Pomfret, CT 06258

Teaching Peace by Red Grammer, Tape available from:
Smilin' Atcha
939 Orchard St.
Peekskill, N.Y. 10566   (914) 739-6275

The Peace Packet
Kids' Records
Box 670, Station A
Toronto, Canada M5W1G3

The Wind Is Telling Secrets, and *Two Hands Hold the Earth*, by Sarah Pirtle, from:
A Gentle Wind
P.O. Box 3103
Albany, N.Y. 12203
(518) 482-9023

Tom Hunter
3212 Northwest Ave. Suite C-321
Bellingham, WA 98225   Phone: (206) 738-0340

Viki Diamond's Tapes of Stories and Songs (A wonderful, must-have resource.)
536 Livingston Street
Westbury, N.Y. 11590   Phone: (516) 333-2381

Books for Adults

Asher, Marty, *Fifty Seven Reasons Not to Have a Nuclear War*, Warner Books, Inc., 1984.

Auvine, Densmore, Extrom, Poole, Shanklin, *A Manual for Group Facilitators*, Center for Conflict Resolution, 731 State Street, Madison, Wisconsin, 1978.

Blood-Patterson, Peter, (editor), *Rise Up Singing*, Sing Out Publications, 1988.

Caduto, Michael and Bruchac, Joseph, *Keepers of the Earth*, Fulcrum, Inc., Golden Colorado, 1988.

Caldicott, Helen, *Nuclear Madness—What Can You Do?* Autumn Press, 1978.

Carlsson-Paige, Nancy, and Levin, Diane E., *Helping Young Children Understand Peace, War, and the Nuclear Threat*, National Association for the Education of Young Children, Washington, D.C., 1985.

Carlsson-Paige, Nancy, and Levin, Diane E., *The War Play Dilemma*, Teachers College Press, Teachers College, Columbia University, New York, 1987.

Carlsson-Paige, Nancy, and Diane E. Levin, *Who's Calling the Shots: How to Respond Effectively to Children's Fascination with War Play and War Toys*, New Society Publishers, Philadelphia, 1989.

Children's Creative Response to Conflict Program, *The Friendly Classroom for a Small Planet,* New Society Publishers, Philadelphia, PA.

Cloud, Deegan, Evans, Imam, Signer, *Watermelons Not War!,* A Support Book for Parenting in the Nuclear Age, Philadelphia, New Society Publishers, 1984.

Crary, Elizabeth, *Kids Can Cooperate*, Parenting Press, 1984.

Derman-Sparks, Louise, with the A. B. C. Task Force, *Anti-Bias Curriculum: Tools for Empowering Young Children*, N.A.E.Y.C., Washington D.C., 1989.

Earthworks Group, *50 Simple Things Kids Can Do To Save the Earth*, Andrews and McMeel N.Y., 1990.

Frank, Jerome D. *Sanity and Survival in the Nuclear Age*, Random House, 1982.

Giono, Jean, *The Man Who Planted Trees*, Chelsea Green Publishing Co., 1985. (A treasure of a book about how one man's inspirational generosity brings regeneration and sanity back to a barren land, reminding us of the importance of living simply.)

I Don't Understand the World Right Now,* Children's comments and drawings from Ithaca, NY. Cornell, University, (607) 256-5187.

Judson, et al, *A Manual On Nonviolence and Children*, New Society Publishers, Philadelphia, PA., 1984.

Keyes, Ken Jr., *The Hundredth Monkey*, Vision Books, 1982.

Kreidler, William J., *Creative Conflict Resolution*, Scott, Foresman & Co., 1984.

La Farge, Phyllis, *Strangelove Legacy*, Harper & Row, 1987.

Lappé, *What To Do After You Turn Off the TV*, Ballantine Books, 1985. Games, ideas, fun and irreverence.

McGinnis, Kathleen and James, *Parenting for Peace and Justice*, Orbis Books, 1981.

Muller, Robert, *New Genesis*, Doubleday & Company, Inc., 1982.

Nagler, Michel N. *America Without Violence*, Island Press, 1982.

Neugebauer, Bonnie, *Alike and Different: Exploring Our Humanity with Young Children,,* Exchange Press, Inc., 1987.

Osada, Arata, *Children of Hiroshima,* Harper and Row, 1982.

Peck, M. Scott, *The Different Drum: Community-Making and Peace,* Simon and Schuster, New York, 1987. (Discussion of the ways groups become communities.)

Scheer, Robert, *With Enough Shovels,* Random House, 1982.

Schell, Jonathan, *The Fate of the Earth,* Alfred Knopf, New York, 1982.

Siegel, Richard, Strassfeld, Michael, Strassfeld, Sharon; *The Jewish Catalog,* The Jewish Publication Society of America, Philadelphia.

Smith, Charles, *Promoting the Social Development of Young Children.**

Sobel, Jeffrey, *Everybody Wins,* Walker & Co., 1983.

Tuchscherer, Pamela, *TV Interactive Toys: The New High Tech Threat to Children,* Pinnaroo Publishing, P.O. Box 7525, Bend, Oregon 97708, 1988.

Vigna, Judith, *Nobody Wants A Nuclear War,* Albert Whitman & Co., 1986.

Warren, Jean & McKinnon, Elizabeth, *Small World Celebrations,* Warren Publishing House, Inc., Everett, Washington, 1988.

* indicates book is possibly out of print. These books can often be found at public libraries.

<u>General Peace Resources</u>

Action for Children's Television
20 University Road
Cambridge, MA 02138

Animal Town Game Company
P.O. Box 20002
Santa Barbara, CA 93120
(805) 682-7343

Berman, Shelley (editor). *Perspectives: A Teaching Guide,* Educators for Social Responsibility, 1983. (This compendium of suggestions, teaching activities, and resource lists is intended for use with students K-12. The wide-ranging subject matter deals with developing in students an active concept and sense of peace independent of its relation to war. A bibliography accompanies each section of the curriculum.)

Bessell, Harold, and Geraldine Ball, *Human Development Program,* Palomares and Associates, P.O. Box 1577, Spring Valley, CA 92077. (The *Magic Circle* program is an oral language approach to life skills which furthers healthy social and emotional growth.)

Beyond War
222 High Street
Palo Alto, CA 94301

Canyon Records
4143 N. 16th Street
Phoenix, AZ 85016
Catalog of Native American music from all tribal areas.

CEASE
c/o Peggy Schirmer
17 Gerry Street
Cambridge, MA 02138

Center for Peace and Conflict Studies
Lillian Genser
Wayne State University
5229 Cass Avenue
Detroit, Michigan 48202

Children's Creative Response to Conflict
Box 271
Nyack, NY 10960
Wrote *The Friendly Classroom for a Small Planet*

Children's Music Network
Sarah Pirtle
54 Thayer Road
Greenfield, MA 01301

Claudia's Caravan
P.O. Box 1582
Alameda, CA 91501
Multicultural bookstore

Co-op America
2100 M Street, N.W.
Suite 403
Washington, D.C. 20063
(Lists companies and products which are socially responsible.)

Cooperative Sports and Games by Terry Orlick, Pantheon Books, N.Y., 1982

Council on Interracial Books for Children
1841 Broadway
New York, NY 10023

Educators For Social Responsibility
23 Garden Street
Cambridge, MA 02138
(617) 492-1764

Fletcher, Ruth, *Teaching Peace: Skills for Living in a Global Society*, Harper and Row Publishers, San Francisco, CA, 1986.

Global Village Toys (Anti-bias products for children, educators, and parents)
2210 Wilshire Blvd. Ste. 262,
Santa Monica, CA, 90403
(213) 459-5188

Institute for Peace and Justice
4144 Lindell, #400
St. Louis, MO 63108
(314) 533-4445

International Child Resource Institute
4360 Lincoln Avenue
Oakland, CA 94062

Jane Adams Children's Book Award
777 United Nations Plaza
New York, NY 10017

Jobs With Peace Education Task Force
10 West Street
Boston, MA 02111

Little Friends for Peace
386 North Cleveland Ave.
St. Paul, MN 55104
(612) 644-8148

National Coalition on Television Violence
P.O. Box 2157
Champaign, IL 61820

Peace Education: A Bibliography for Young Children
Rosmarie Greiner
126 Escalona
Santa Cruz, CA 95060
(Highly Recommended)

Peace Links Missouri
6800 Washington Avenue
St. Louis, MO 63130
Dolores Kirk (314) 727-2273

Peaceworks
P.O. Box 275
Cape Porpoise, ME 04014

Prutzman, Stern, Burger, Bodenhamer, *The Friendly Classroom for a Small Planet, A Handbook on Creative Approaches to Living and Problem-solving for Children*, New Society Publishers, Santa Cruz, CA.

Pueblo to People—catalog of Central American items
A Non-profit Organization
1616 Montrose #3100
Houston, TX 77006

Reardon, Betty A., *Educating for a Global Responsibility: Teacher-Designed Curricula for Peace Education*, (K-12), Teachers College Press, Teachers College, Columbia University, New York, 1987.

Schmidt, Fran and Friedman, Alice, *Peace Making Skills for Little Kids*, from Peace Works.

Skipping Stones: A multi-ethnic children's forum
(505) 942-9434.

Stop War Toys Campaign
New England War Resisters League
Box 1093
Norwich, CT 06360
(203) 889-5337

Storytelling
NAPPS
P.O. Box 309
Jonesborough, TN 37659

Strickland, Dorothy, *Listen Children: an Anthology of Black Literature*, Bantam Books, New York, 1982.

The Beyond War Classroom: Peace Building from Person to Planet—an integrated arts curriculum for preschool and kindergarten by Beth London, (802) 899-3716.

United Nations Gift Shops
Consult local directories

Wilmington College Peace Resource Center
Pyle Center Box 1183
Wilmington, OH 45177

Women's International League for Peace and Freedom
1213 Race Street
Philadelphia, PA 19107